Abingdon's

Bible Zone®

Where the Bible Comes to Life

Older Elementary 7

New Life

Also available from Abingdon Press:

Abingdon's BibleZone®
Preschool 7
Teacher's Guide

Abingdon's BibleZone®
Preschool 7
FUNspirational® Kit

Abingdon's BibleZone®
Younger Elementary 7
Teacher's Guide

Abingdon's BibleZone®
Younger Elementary 7
FUNspirational® Kit

Abingdon's BibleZone®
Older Elementary 7
FUNspirational® Kit

Writer/Editor: Judy Newman-St. John
Story Writer: Dr. Michael E. Williams
Bible Background: LeeDell Stickler
Production Editor: Betsi Hoey Smith
Production and Design Manager:
R. E. Osborne
Designer: Paige Easter
Front Cover Photo: Ron Benedict
Back Cover Photo: Ron Benedict
Illustrator: Jim Padgett
Illustrator: Charles Jakubowski
Illustrator: Megan Jeffrey

Abingdon's

Bible ZONE ®

Older Elementary

7

Where the Bible Comes to Life

NEW LIFE

Abingdon Press
Nashville

Abingdon's
BibleZone®
Where the Bible Comes to Life
Older Elementary 7

Art Credits:
Pages 16, 20, 28, 32, 76, 80, 90, 100, 102, 104, 116, 140: Jim Padgett, © 1999 Abingdon Press.
Pages 44, 56, 68, 92, 128, 152, and 164: Charles Jakubowski, © 1999 Abingdon Press.
Pages 52, 66, 88, 126, and 160: Megan Jeffery, © 1999 Abingdon Press.

99 00 01 02 03 04 05 06 07 08—10 9 8 7 6 5 4 3 2 1
MANUFACTURED IN THE UNITED STATES OF AMERICA

Table of Contents

New Life

Bible Units in the

New Life in Jesus

Bible Story	Bible Verse
Shout Hosanna!	Mark 11:9
Remember Me	Luke 22:19
Road to the Cross	Matthew 27:54
Jesus Lives!	Luke 24:5
Do You Believe?	John 20:29

New Life in God's World

Bible Story	Bible Verse
In the Beginning	Psalm 8:1
Sun, Moon, Stars	Psalm 19:1
All God's Creatures	Psalm 104:24
In God's Image	Genesis 1:27
Adam and Eve	Psalm 100:3
The Naming	Psalm 8:6
Trouble in Paradise	Genesis 2:16-17
For Everything a Season	Ecclesiastes 3:1

BIBLEZONE®

About Bible ZONE®

ZoneZillies®:

ZoneZillies® are game and storytelling props found in the BibleZone® FUNspirational® Kit. Some ZoneZillies® are consumable and will need to be replaced. These are added for the teacher's convenience.

- fun loop straws
- plastic eggs
- bouncing rock balls
- ping pong balls
- paper blow-outs
- growing animals
- balloons
- inflatable celestial ball

- earth kickballs
- white yarn
- yellow yarn
- atom balls
- night sky stickers
- creature kickballs
- Cassette with music by Brentwood Kids Music

Supplies:

- Bible for each student
- cassette player
- index cards
- construction paper
- paste or glue
- scissors
- clear tape & masking tape
- crayons, markers, pencils
- tempera paint & brushes
- large pieces of paper
- stapler, staples
- nature magazines
- newspapers
- wrapping paper
- blindfolds
- brown paper bag
- paper plates & napkins
- basket, trash can or box
- corks, needles, safety pins
- cotton balls and baby oil
- milk
- frozen limeade concentrate
- plastic container with lid
- resealable plastic bags
- cardboard or heavy paper

- flour, salt
- water
- bowls, clear plastic cups
- squeeze bottles, spray bottles
- various kinds of bread
- plastic knives, large spoons
- margarine or softened butter
- honey
- flat sheet, black bed sheet
- pennies or paper clips
- seven candles
- feathers
- wide-mouth quart jars with lids
- small gravel, sand, soil, charcoal chips, dead leaves or peat moss
- small wild plants
- 10-ounce plastic soft drink bottles with lids
- ink pads with washable ink
- small sponges
- concordance
- various kinds of decorative paper
- shoebox lids or posterboard
- tissue paper
- old pantihose, wire coat hangers

7

Welcome to the Bible ZONE®

Where the Bible Comes to Life

Have fun learning about favorite Bible stories from the Old and New Testaments. Each lesson in this teacher guide is filled with games and activities that will make learning FUNspirational® for you and your students. With just a few added supplies, everything you need to teach is included in the Abingdon's BibleZone® FUNspirational® Kit.

Each lesson has a ZoneIn® box:

> **God wants us to share our gifts and talents with others.**

that is repeated over and over again throughout the lesson.
The ZoneIn® states the Bible message in words your students will connect to their lives.

Use the following tips to help make your trip into the BibleZone® a FUNspirational® success!
- Read through each lesson. Read the Bible passages.
- Memorize the Bible verse and the ZoneIn® statement.
- Choose the activities that fit your unique group of students and your time limitations.
- Read great storytelling tips in the article on pages 171 and 172.
- Practice telling the BibleZone® story.
- Gather the ZoneZillies® you will use for the lesson.
- Gather supplies you will use for the lesson.
- Learn the music for the lesson from the BibleZone® FUNspirational® Cassette.
- Arrange your room space so there is plenty of room for the students to move and sit on the floor.
- Photocopy the Reproducible pages for the lesson.
- Photocopy the HomeZone® page for students.
- Photocopy the nametags (p. 173) and the words to the song "The Bible Zone" (p. 174) for each student.

Older Elementary

Each child in your class is a one-of-a-kind child of God. Each child has his or her own name, background, family situation, and set of experiences. It is important to remember and celebrate the uniqueness of each child. Yet all of these one-of-a-kind children of God have some common needs.

- All children need love.
- All children need a sense of self-worth.
- All children need to feel a sense of accomplishment.
- All children need to have a safe place to be and express their feelings.
- All children need to be surrounded by adults who love them.
- All children need to experience the love of God.

Older Elementary students (ages 9–12 years old) also have some common characteristics.

Their Bodies

- They are experiencing rapid physical and emotional changes.
- Their growing takes a lot of energy, sometimes leaving them lethargic.
- There are great variations of emotional and physical growth among older elementary age students. They are different from one another and different from who they were just a short time ago.

Their Minds

- They are concrete thinkers.
- They are practical planners, working toward logical conclusions.
- They like to identify and express attitudes, ideas, and feelings about unfairness and unjust treatment of people.
- They like to laugh and can be silly.
- They are ready for challenging Bible skills and activities.
- They are ready to increase and use vocabulary related to the Christian faith.
- They are capable of understanding people and places unknown to them.

Their Relationships

- They desire to be similar to all their friends but recognize they are not.
- They may have trouble accepting themselves and others at different stages of their personal development.
- They adopt adult language and can appear to be sophisticated.
- They do not want to appear to be vulnerable or innocent.
- They are beginning to identify themselves as individuals separate from their families.

Their Hearts

- They need caring adults who model Christian attitudes and behaviors.
- They need to verbalize experiences and questions about God and faith.
- They need to serve with others in the community and the world.
- They need to feel they have a personal relationship with God.
- They need a sense of belonging to the church and to the larger faith community.

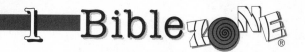

Shout Hosanna!

Enter the

Bible Verse

Hosanna! Blessed is the one who comes in the name of the Lord!

Mark 11:9

Bible Story

Matthew 21:1-11; Mark 11:1-10; Luke 19:28-40; John 12:12-16

For centuries the Jewish people had looked for the coming of the Messiah whom God would send to save their nation. They remembered the prophecy of Zechariah, who told of the king who would come to save God's people. When Jesus entered Jerusalem, some of the people gave Jesus a conqueror's welcome, greeting him as the King of Israel. The clothing and branches the people put in Jesus' path were signs of honor.

The crowds were exuberant. What we now know as Holy Week began with praise and celebration. But quickly it changed to rejection and denial.

When Jesus entered Jerusalem, the people expected their Messiah to come in the form of a strong military leader who would overthrow the Roman government. The Messiah would be, of course, from King David's lineage. But Jesus didn't fulfill their expectations. He came riding a lowly donkey instead of a horse. And his message of change was through love and compassion, not through military might.

Some of the religious leaders were watching as Jesus entered their city. Some of the priests, scribes, and elders must have been angry and determined to bring down the man they considered an imposter or a rebel leader.

Your students may be experiencing intense emotions that often come with adolescence. Some may have unrealistic expectations of themselves. Others may have relatives who expect too much. Some may struggle with impossible expectations of others. Some may identify with Jesus, who was misunderstood. They may be ready for a new relationship with God. Help your students know that through Jesus, we all can have new beginnings and new life.

We praise God for Jesus, who brings new life.

Scope the ZONE

ZONE	TIME	SUPPLIES	⊚ ZILLIES
Zoom Into the Zone			
Get in the Zone	5 minutes	pages 173 and 174, cassette player, pens or markers, safety pins or tape	Cassette
Persnickety Pathways	10 minutes	Reproducible 1C, tape, paper marker	yarn
Surprise!	10 minutes	scissors	yarn
BibleZone®			
Zoom Into the Bible	15 minutes	Bible for each student	none
Enjoy the Story	15 minutes	Reproducibles 1A and 1B	none
LifeZone			
Piquage, Please!	15 minutes	Reproducible 1D, corks, needles, bright crayons, cotton balls, baby oil, newspaper	none
Shake Hosanna	10 minutes	milk, frozen limeade concentrate, plastic container with lid, clear plastic cups, resealable plastic bags	fun loop straws
Sing	5 minutes	Reproducible 1E, cassette player	Cassette
Echo Praise	5 minutes	none	none

⊚ Zillies® are found in the **BibleZone® FUNspirational® Kit.**

Zoom Into the Zone

Choose one or more activities to catch your children's interest.

Get in the Zone

Supplies:
pages 173 and 174, cassette player, pens or markers, safety pins or tape

Zillies®:
Cassette

Have "The Bible Zone" **(Cassette)** playing as the students enter the room. Greet each student enthusiastically and **say: Welcome to the Bible Zone, the fun place where the Bible comes alive!**

If the students do not know one another, give them nametags to wear **(page 173).** Give each student a copy of the words to "The Bible Zone" **(page 174).** Play the song again and invite everyone to sing with you.

Persnickety Pathways

Supplies:
Reproducible 1C, tape, paper, marker

Zillies®:
none

Make several copies of the palm pattern **(Reproducible 1C).** Use the palms to create an obvious but challenging path to follow by taping them to the floor, walls, underside of a table, back of chairs, and on other obstacles. Place enough distance between the palms that the students can reach them by extending a hand or foot from one to the next. Place a sign that says "Welcome to Jerusalem" at the end of the path.

Invite the students to take turns traveling the path. Keep time for each student. Be sure the students know they must touch each palm with a hand or foot. If you have a large class, divide the students into teams of two or three to travel the path together. Have members of each team hold onto one another's wrists as they travel.

Say: When Jesus entered Jerusalem, people were so happy to see him that they cheered and spread palm branches on the road.

Surprise!

Supplies:
scissors

Zillies®:
yarn

Ask each student to cut a length of **yarn.** (Do not suggest a length.) When everyone has a length, ask each student to tell one thing about himself or herself for every time the yarn can be wrapped around his or her finger. **Ask: What surprises did you hear about one another? What things were different than you expected?**

Say: When Jesus entered Jerusalem, the people were looking for a great military leader to save them. They were surprised to learn that Jesus wasn't exactly the kind of king they were expecting.

12

 Bible **ZONE**

Choose one or more activities to immerse your children in the Bible story.

Zoom Into the Bible

Supplies:
Bible for each student

Zillies®:
none

Be certain each student has a Bible. Divide the students into four teams. (For ideas of ways to create teams, see page 167.) Ask Team One to read Matthew 21:1-11. Ask Team Two to read Mark 11:1-10. Ask Team Three to read Luke 19:28-40. Ask Team Four to read John 12:12-16.

Say: Matthew, Mark, Luke, and John are the four Gospels. They each record stories about Jesus. The stories are the same with some slight differences. Let's look at the story of the triumphal entry and see what the differences are.

Ask:
1. What did Jesus ask the disciples to do? (*Matthew—go into the village, find a donkey and colt, and bring them to Jesus; Mark and Luke—bring a colt that has never been ridden; John—is not included*)
2. What were the disciples to say if anyone said anything to them? (*Matthew, Mark, Luke—The Lord needs them; John—is not included.*)
3. What did the crowds do when Jesus entered Jerusalem? (*Matthew and Mark—laid their cloaks and branches from the trees on the road; Luke—cloaks; John—branches*)
4. What word did the crowds shout at Jesus? (*Matthew, Mark, John—Hosanna!*)
5. What did they call Jesus? (*Matthew—Son of David, the one who comes in the name of the Lord; Mark and John—the one; Luke—the king*)

Enjoy the Story

Supplies:
Reproducibles 1A and 1B

Zillies®:
none

Tell or read the story "The Holy Week Whodunit, Part 1" (**Reproducibles 1A and 1B**). For helpful storytelling hints, read the article on **pages 171-172**.

Ask: What do you think it was like when Jesus entered Jerusalem? Do you think anyone in the crowd wanted to kill Jesus even then?

Say: We will continue the story for the next few weeks. I think we will all be surprised when we find out whodunit.

The Holy Week Whodunit
(Part 1)

by Michael E. Williams

Ms. Porter told the class that they were going to have a special project going through Lent. She explained that Lent began on Ash Wednesday and continued through Holy Week, forty days if you didn't include Sundays. There was a special reason not to include Sundays.

There were six Sundays *in* Lent. She explained that they were *in* Lent not *of* Lent because they were not really counted as part of the season. Lent was a time when people gave up things. Sometimes they gave up food for a day, called fasting. Or they gave up a particular food or activity for the entire time of Lent. Since Sundays were days that the Church remembered Jesus' resurrection, they were always considered feast days. Sundays were not really considered to be a part of a season of giving up things.

The word *Lent,* Ms. Porter explained, was not really religious in its origin. It came from an Early English word that referred to the lengthening of the days during the Spring. She also told her fifth and sixth grade students that Lent along with Easter and Pentecost were the parts of the Christian Year that had been observed the longest.

"In our class during the Sundays in Lent we will be studying the Holy Week story. Each Sunday we will take an incident from that story and learn as much as possible about it," Ms. Porter told her students.

Felix raised his hand and when his teacher called on him, he asked, "Will there be a test?" Felix usually made comments he thought were funny.

"No, Felix," Ms. Porter responded, smiling. "There won't be a test. But there is a question I want you to answer. It's kind of a mystery."

"A mystery? Oh boy!" Jasmine blurted out. "I love mysteries."

"Well, this is not an easy one, though it may appear to be on the surface." Ms. Porter looked serious now. "We are all going to become detectives and see if we can discover who is responsible for Jesus' death."

Several hands went up and voices from different parts of the room began to shout, "I know. I know."

"Not so fast," Ms. Porter motioned for them to lower their hands. "We'll discover the answer together as we work through the stories."

They began with the story of Jesus entering Jerusalem. Brenda, Sean, and May Lin read the Bible aloud. While the different Gospels told it a little differently, the general gist of the story was this: that Jesus came into Jerusalem riding on a donkey, people shouted "Hosanna," waved their palm branches, and threw their cloaks down in front of the donkey.

"Why would he ride on a donkey?" Ms. Porter asked the class.

"Because he couldn't afford a limousine," Felix quipped.

Reproducible 1A

"Not exactly." Ms. Porter tried not to encourage his cute answers.

"Everybody knows there were no limousines in those days." Brenda gave Felix a hard look.

"Let's get back to the question." Ms. Porter held a hand out toward Felix as if to say—don't respond to Brenda. He started to say something, but didn't.

May Lin spoke up. "If he rode a horse, it would make him look too much like a soldier."

"Why didn't he want to look like a soldier?" asked the teacher.

"Because he's the Prince of Peace," Jasmine responded. "You can't have the Prince of Peace going around looking like the Prince of War."

"That's true, Jasmine." Ms. Porter smiled. "Many people thought the Messiah would be a military leader who would overthrow the Romans and establish Jewish rule in Jerusalem again. They expected it to be like the good old days when King David reigned. Since Jesus wasn't that kind of Messiah, he didn't want to give people the impression that he was going to be a military leader. Why else?"

"Because some prophet said he would ride a donkey." This time it was Sean who spoke.

"Very good, Sean. The Gospel writers were very interested in how Jesus fit into some of the writings of the Hebrew prophets. Now, how did the people respond to Jesus coming into town riding on a donkey?" Ms. Porter was hoping to move the discussion right along.

Brenda answered, "They threw their coats down in front of him and waved palm branches and shouted 'Hosanna!'"

"Was that a good thing or a bad thing? I mean, did they approve of Jesus or not?" Ms. Porter probed.

"Approved," May Lin jumped in.

"How do you know?" their teacher asked.

"Because they all seemed to be happy about it, treating him like he was someone important?" Sean's answer sounded like a question. This only meant that he wasn't sure it was right.

"Correct," was the teacher's quick response. "In that case who would want to kill Jesus?"

"Nobody," said several students.

"Well, maybe the people whose coats his donkey stepped on and got dirty," Felix grinned.

"Then they shouldn't have thrown them down in front of him in the first place," was Brenda's comeback.

"Jesus has already told his disciples that he will have to suffer and die. How do you think he feels now?" Ms. Porter could tell by her watch that they were almost out of time.

"Like maybe it won't happen after all," answered Sean.

"Like the people are happy now but that they will turn against him when they find out he's not a soldier," said Jasmine.

"Like maybe he wanted to get off the donkey and give his bottom a rest." This, of course, was Felix.

Just so the class clown wouldn't have the last word Ms. Porter told them, "We'll work on the story some more next week. Now, it's time to find your parents and go to worship."

Reproducible 1B

Reproducible 1C

BIBLEZONE®

Piquage, Please!

Supplies:
Reproducible 1D, corks, needles, bright crayons, cotton balls, baby oil, newspaper

Zillies®:
none

(P) repare for each student a cork that has a needle pushed into it so that the blunt end of the needle is sticking out of the cork. Give each student a photocopy of the stained glass window (**Reproducible 1D**) and a cork and needle.

Say: We are going to use an art technique called piquage. Carefully use the blunt end of the needle to push holes all around the frame of the window. You should go slowly and carefully so that the paper is not torn. When you finish, the window will be completely punched out of the paper, and the edge of it will look feathery.

Invite the students to use bright crayons to color the stained glass. Then have the students place the picture on newspaper and rub a cotton ball that has some baby oil on it over the picture. When the oil has dried, the stained glass windows will have a shiny finish.

Shake Hosanna

Supplies:
milk, frozen limeade concentrate, plastic container with lid, clear plastic cups, resealable plastic bags

Zillies®:
fun loop straws

(P) our 1 quart milk and 1 6-ounce frozen limeade concentrate into a plastic container with a lid. Make sure the lid is securely fastened.

Let the students take turns shaking the container until the milk and limeade are mixed together. Have each student repeat the Bible verse, "Hosanna! Blessed is the one who comes in the name of the Lord!" (Mark 11:9) as they shake the mixture.

Pour into clear plastic cups. Give each student a **fun loop straw.** Let the students enjoy their shakes. Have each student rinse the straw and place it inside a resealable plastic bag. Have each student write her or his name on the plastic bag. The fun loop straws will be used again in other lessons.

Note: Makes nine to ten servings.

Supplies:
Reproducible 1E,
cassette player

Zillies®:
Cassette

Sing

Give each student a copy of the words to the song "Amazing Grace" **(Reproducible 1E)**. Ask everyone to follow along reading the words as you play the song on the **Cassette**. Play the song again and invite everyone to sing.

Supplies:
none

Zillies®:
none

Echo Praise

Ask the students to stand in a circle with you. **Say: Our Bible verse for today is Mark 11:9, "Hosanna! Blessed is the one who comes in the name of the Lord!"** The word *Hosanna!* means "a cry of worshipful praise" and comes from the Hebrew word *Hoshana,* which means "save us."

Invite the students to repeat today's verse with you. Invite them to join you in the following litany by **saying: Please echo the words I say the same way I say them, and do the gestures I do.**

Hosanna! *(loudly, waving arms overhead)*
Blessed *(softly, hands folded in prayer)*
Hosanna! *(loudly, waving arms overhead)*
Blessed is the one *(firmly, hands folded in prayer on* Blessed, *and raising one arm and pointing finger up on* one)
Blessed is the one *(repeat motions)*
who comes in the name of the Lord! *(On* comes, *hold both palms up and sweep arms in front of you from right to left. On* name, *touch fingers on both hands to your lips. On* Lord, *hold both arms up with elbows bent, palms open.)*
Blessed *(softly, hands folded in prayer)*
Hosanna! *(loudly, waving arms overhead)*

Pray: Dear God, we thank you and praise you for your Son, Jesus. We know that Jesus saved us and brings us new life. We thank you for each new day and for each new opportunity to know you and to live as you want us to live. Amen.

**We praise God for Jesus,
who brings new life.**

Give each student a copy of HomeZone® to enjoy this week.

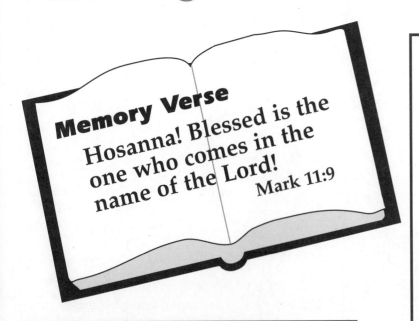

Memory Verse

Hosanna! Blessed is the one who comes in the name of the Lord!

Mark 11:9

Caramel Corn

You will need:
2 cups firmly packed light brown sugar
1 cup butter
1 teaspoon salt
½ cup light corn syrup
1 teaspoon baking soda
6 quarts popped popcorn

Combine the first four ingredients in a heavy saucepan. Bring to a boil and stir occasionally for 5 minutes. Remove from heat and stir in baking soda. Pour over popcorn. Stir until coated. Spread on a large cookie sheet or in a large roasting pan.

Bake at 200 degrees for 60 minutes, stirring every 15 minutes. Remove from oven and let cool. Makes 6 quarts.

Plant People!

Spring is the perfect time for planting. You can make a funny plant person to help you celebrate spring!

You will need an old nylon stocking, sawdust (or vermiculite, perlite, or soil), two tablespoons of grass seed, scissors, and a twist tie.

Cut the foot from the stocking, about where the ankle would be. Pour the grass seed into the toe of the stocking. Add sawdust until the foot is full. Gather the opening of the stocking tightly, and tie it closed with a twist tie. Shape the stocking into a round head.

Place the round head of your plant person on a saucer with the twist tie down. Place your plant in a sunny spot and soak it with water every day. Before long your plant person will have lots of green hair for you to cut! Pin on paper eyes, nose, mouth, and moustache, if you wish!

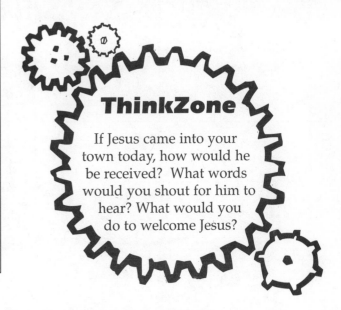

ThinkZone

If Jesus came into your town today, how would he be received? What words would you shout for him to hear? What would you do to welcome Jesus?

Zone In

We praise God for Jesus, who brings new life.

Reproducible 1D

Amazing Grace

Amazing grace! How sweet the sound
That saved a wretch like me!
I once was lost, but now am found,
Was blind but now I see.

Thru many dangers, toils and snares,
I have already come;
Tis grace has brought me safe thus far,
and grace will lead me home.

'Twas grace that taught my heart to fear,
and grace my fears relieved;
How precious did that grace appear
the hour I first believed.

Amazing! Amazing! Amazing! Oh, yeah!

When we've been there ten thousand years,
bright shining as the sun,
We've no less days to sing God's praise
than when we'd first begun.

Writers: Troy and Genie Nilsson
Publisher: Bridge Building Music
Copyright © 1995 Bridge Building Music/BMI
All Rights Reserved.
Used by permission of Brentwood-Benson Music Publishing, Inc.
From the Brentwood-Benson Music Publishing, Inc. recording *Hymns in the House*.

Reproducible 1 E

Remember Me

Enter the

Bible Verse

This is my body, which is given for you.
Do this in remembrance of me.

Luke 22:19

Bible Story

Matthew 26:17-19, 26-30; Mark 14:12-16, 22-25; Luke 22:7-20

Jesus and his friends came to Jerusalem to celebrate the Passover. The people greeted them with great hosannas. But now preparations had to be made to celebrate the traditional Passover meal.

Using a Jewish custom, a rabbi sharing bread and wine with his pupils, Jesus took elements of the Seder, the Passover meal, and established what is today known as the sacrament of the Lord's Supper or Holy Communion.

Bread was an ancient symbol of God's blessings. The unleavened bread at Passover has reminded centuries of Jews of the haste in which their ancestors had left Egypt—so quickly that their bread had no time to rise. The shedding of blood was understood by ancient peoples as the very essence of life.

In what must have been an emotional time, Jesus asked the disciples to eat the bread. He told them it was a symbol of his body, which would be broken for them. Then he took the traditional cup of blessing and asked them to drink of it, calling it a sym-bol of his blood, which would be shed for them. He told them that whenever they gathered to share bread and wine, they should remember him as they did so.

At the Last Supper Jesus warned his disciples that he would be betrayed and that he would die. In Jesus' death God would make a new covenant with the people, a covenant of salvation from the slavery of sin and death.

Help your students understand that during Communion we come together to remember. Communion is an act of remembering—remembering Jesus' sacrifice for us, remembering his Last Supper, and remembering the times we have gathered with other Christians to celebrate the holy meal.

We remember Jesus and thank God for the new life Jesus brings.

Scope the ZONE

ZONE	TIME	SUPPLIES	⊚ ZILLIES®
Zoom Into the Zone			
Get in the Zone	5 minutes	pages 173 and 174, safety pins or tape, cassette player	Cassette
Run 'n Remember	15 minutes	Reproducible 2D, scissors, tape, chairs, cassette player	Cassette
BibleZone®			
Zoom Into the Bible	15 minutes	Bible for each student	none
Enjoy the Story	15 minutes	Reproducibles 2A and 2B	none
LifeZone			
Puff 'n Shine	10 minutes	Reproducible 2C, scissors, pencils, cardboard or heavy paper, white glue, gray and brown liquid tempera paint, paintbrushes, flour, salt, water, bowls, plastic squeeze bottles	none
Glorious Bread	5 minutes	various kinds of bread (see page 30); plastic knives, margarine or softened butter, honey, small paper plates, napkins	none
Egg-citing Egg Race	10 minutes	paper, pen, scissors	plastic eggs
Sing	5 minutes	Reproducible 2E, cassette player	Cassette
Praise	5 minutes	none	none

⊚ Zillies® are found in the **BibleZone® FUNspirational® Kit.**

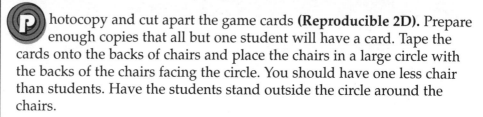

Choose one or more activities to catch your children's interest.

Supplies:

pages 173 and 174, safety pins or tape, cassette player

Zillies®:

Cassette

Get in the Zone

Have "The Bible Zone" **(Cassette)** playing as the students enter the room. Greet each student enthusiastically and **say: Welcome to the Bible Zone, the fun place where the Bible comes alive!**

If the students do not know one another, give them nametags to wear **(page 173)**. Give each student a copy of the words to "The Bible Zone" **(page 174)**. Play the song again and invite everyone to sing with you.

Supplies:

Reproducible 2D, scissors, tape, chairs, cassette player

Zillies®:

Cassette

Run 'n Remember ✓

Photocopy and cut apart the game cards **(Reproducible 2D)**. Prepare enough copies that all but one student will have a card. Tape the cards onto the backs of chairs and place the chairs in a large circle with the backs of the chairs facing the circle. You should have one less chair than students. Have the students stand outside the circle around the chairs.

Say: I will play music from the Cassette. As the music plays, run around the outside of the chairs. When I stop the music, sit on a chair facing the circle! Whoever is left standing must come inside the circle, take one of the cards off a chair, and tell us a story. Your story should tell us about someone the picture on the card reminds you of. Your story can be real or made up, funny or sad! Begin your story by saying, "I remember . . ."

Begin the game. After a student has told a story, have him or her return to the circle and begin play again. Continue play until all the cards have been used.

Say: We often remember people for different reasons. Sometimes we remember them because they were funny or brave or very important. Jesus gave us something special to remember and a special way to remember him. Let's find out what that way was.

 We remember Jesus and thank God for the new life Jesus brings.

Bible ONE

Choose one or more activities to immerse your children in the Bible story.

Zoom Into the Bible

(D) ivide the students into three teams. Ask Team One to read Matthew 26:17-19 and 26-30. Ask Team Two to read Mark 14:12-16 and 22-25. Ask Team Three to read Luke 22:7-20.

Ask the teams to share what they have read in the Scriptures. **Ask: What did Jesus give us to remember?** *(a new covenant)* **How did Jesus give us the new covenant to remember?** *(He said that the bread and the cup should be symbols of his body and blood.)*

Say: A covenant is a promise between people or between people and God. In the Old Testament we find that God made a covenant with Abraham and Sarah. God promised to give Abraham and Sarah many descendants and to give Abraham's family a land of their own. Abraham and Sarah promised to worship God. Later in the Old Testament God renewed the covenant with the Hebrew people through Moses and the Ten Commandments. God promised to give the people a land of their own. The people promised that they would follow God's laws.

Say: The new covenant that Jesus talked about was a covenant based not upon obeying laws, but upon acting in love. Because of Jesus' life and Jesus' sacrifice, we can have a new relationship with God.

Say: Jesus knew that it probably would be the last time he and his friends would be together, and he wanted to share the celebration of the Passover with them. Jesus wanted the disciples to remember what he had been teaching them about God and about living as God's people. So he picked two foods that all of them ate every day—bread and wine—and asked them to remember him whenever they ate and drank these foods. Jesus compared the bread to his body and the wine to his blood, and these two foods have become the symbols used in Holy Communion in the church today.

Supplies:
Bible for each student

Zillies®:
none

Enjoy the Story

(T) ell or read the story "The Holy Week Whodunit, Part 2" **(Reproducibles 2A and 2B).** For helpful storytelling hints, read the article on **pages 171-172..**

Ask: Who do you think killed Jesus?

Supplies:
Reproducibles 2A and 2B

Zillies®:
none

The Holy Week Whodunit
(Part 2)

by Michael E. Williams

When Ms. Porter's students came into her room, nothing was the same as it had been before. Was this a part of the mystery they were trying to solve? Were there clues hidden in the new way the room was arranged? They would soon find out.

All the chairs were missing and the tables were out of place. In fact, the tables weren't even standing up on their legs. No, the legs were folded under them, and the tables sat on short blocks just a few inches above the floor. They were arranged in the shape of the letter "U" and there were pillows all around the outside of the letter.

Ms. Porter invited the class in and asked them to take a seat around the outside of the "U."

"You have been invited to a very special meal,"Ms. Porter said. "Jesus requests your presence at his last supper with his disciples. In fact, you will be the disciples. This is the sort of table they would have sat around most likely. At this table you lie on the floor with your feet pointed away from the table. In those days people would have rested on their left elbows and eaten with their right hands."

Felix was the first to chime in, "Great, we get to eat with our hands. Look, there is no silverware on the table."

"You'll be instructed on how to eat in just a minute." Ms. Porter continued with her lesson. "Most scholars think that the meal would have been a Passover meal. This means that they would have eaten certain foods and told a particular story. Do you remember last year when Rabbi Roth came and shared the Seder meal with our congregation? What story did he tell during the meal?"

"When the slaves came out of Egypt," May Lin said. "What's the name for it?"

"The Exodus," her teacher answered.

"And we had to taste horseradish. It tasted terrible," Sean remembered out loud.

"Those were the bitter herbs to remind us how bitter slavery in Egypt was," Jasmine told him. "My people were slaves once in this country, and I've read books about how terrible that was. I remember there was salt-water for the tears of the slaves, and we dipped a boiled egg into it."

"What else do you remember?" Ms. Porter asked.

"There was that flat bread kind of like hard crackers. The rabbi hid a piece of it, and we got to look for it," answered Sean.

"Matzo or unleavened bread. Does anybody remember why it is flat instead of soft and puffy?" Their teacher prodded their memories.

"Because they were in such a hurry to get out of Egypt that they didn't have time to let their bread rise," Jasmine spoke up.

Reproducible 2A

BibleZone®

"Exactly," her teacher smiled. "What else?"

"My little sister got to ask why this night was different from all other nights because she was the youngest one there," May Lin responded. "And we all liked the sweet stuff we dipped the bread in."

"Haroset, made from fruit and nuts and honey. That was good, wasn't it?"Ms. Porter agreed.

Felix ended the discussion of the Seder meal with, "And we didn't have to lie down in the floor to eat it."

"Right you are," said his teacher. "Let's read in our Bibles what happened at that meal with Jesus and his disciples. You may just get a clue to the mystery I asked you about last time."

When they had read the story, their teacher began to ask questions again. "Imagine that you are one of the disciples gathered around the table that night. How do you think you would feel when Jesus said that one of you would betray him?"

"Terrible," Sean said. "I would keep thinking whether I was the one. Could I do something like that to somebody who was supposed to be my friend?"

"I guess any of them, I mean us, could have done it." Brenda looked at all the others.

"Judas did it," May Lin asked, "didn't he?"

"Jesus said the one who dipped the bread into the dish with him did it," Sean looked to his teacher.

"That's what he said," Ms. Porter answered.

"And that was Judas? Right?" Sean was pursuing an idea. Everyone could see it on his face.

"That's right, Sean. Does anyone remember how much he was paid to turn Jesus in?" Ms. Porter asked.

"Thirty pieces of silver," Jasmine gave the answer.

"So, if Judas turned Jesus in, then he would be to blame for Jesus' death. Right?" Sean was on a roll. "So, I've solved the mystery. Judas is the one who killed Jesus."

"Some people think that you're right, that Judas should bear the blame for Jesus' death. It's very possible that he blamed himself in that way. One story even says that he killed himself after trying to give the thirty pieces of silver back." Ms Porter seemed to be supporting Sean's solution.

"He even kissed Jesus to show the soldiers who to arrest," Sean added. "That proves that Judas is to blame. Doesn't it?"

"But there was a trial. Judas didn't hold the trial, did he?" Brenda seemed to be casting doubt on Sean's conclusion.

"And the judge was a guy who flew a plane," Felix proclaimed.

"The judge was Pontius Pilate; that's P I L A T E, not P I L O T," Ms. Porter corrected. "I have an idea. Over the next two weeks let's read over the story of the trial and have a debate to see if Judas or Pilate or someone else might have been responsible for Jesus execution."

Everyone agreed that it was a great idea and started to work.

Reproducible 2B

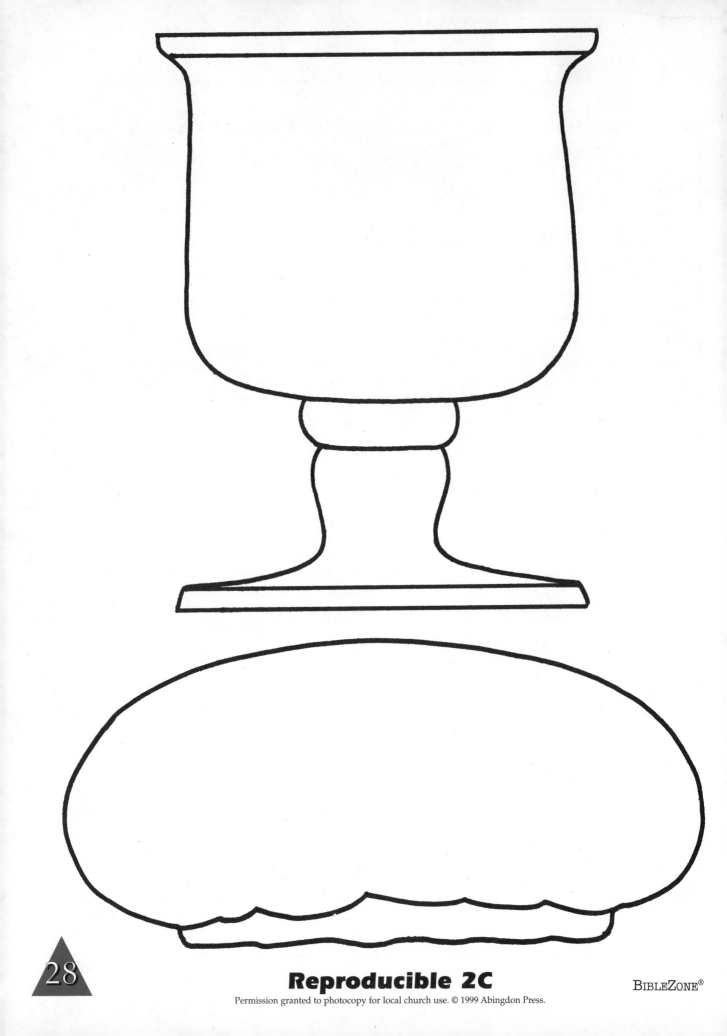

Reproducible 2C

BIBLEZONE®

Choose one or more activities to bring the Bible to life.

Puff 'n Shine

Give each student a photocopy of the bread and chalice pattern **(Reproducible 2C).** Ask each student to cut out the pattern and trace it onto a piece of cardboard or heavy paper.

Prepare shiny paint by mixing white glue and gray liquid tempera paint (or combine black and white tempera paint to create gray). Use a brush to carefully paint the chalice using the shiny paint.

Prepare brown puffy paint by mixing equal parts of flour, salt, and water in a bowl. Add brown liquid tempera paint (or combine red and black tempera paint to create brown) to create a light brown color. Pour the paint into plastic squeeze bottles. Squeeze the paint to cover the bread. The paint will harden in a puffy shape.

When dry, glaze the entire painting with white glue thinned with water for an extra layer of clear glaze.

Say: We express our thanks to God when we celebrate Holy Communion today. We accept the bread and wine as symbols of Jesus and how Jesus sacrificed his life so that we can freely accept God's forgiveness.

Supplies:
Reproducible 2C, scissors, pencils, cardboard or heavy paper, white glue, gray and brown liquid tempera paint, paintbrushes, flour, salt, water, bowls, plastic squeeze bottles

Zillies®:
none

Glorious Bread

Place the various kinds of bread on the table.

Ask: Are there any breads here that you do not recognize? Are there breads here that you especially like?

Say: In Bible times, everyone ate bread. Even the poorest families had bread as a part of their meals. Bread was never cut with a knife; it was always broken.

Share the different kinds of bread with the students. Let them taste as many varieties as you have. Do not force any student to eat.

Say: Every country today has bread in one form or another. When Jesus used bread as a special way of remembering, he knew it was something that people could do easily.

Supplies:
various kinds of bread (white, wheat, bagels, matzoh, baguette, tortilla, rice, rye, bread sticks), plastic knives, margarine or softened butter, honey, small paper plates, napkins

Zillies®:

Supplies:
paper, pen, scissors

Zillies®:
plastic eggs

Egg-citing Egg Race

Prepare two sets of **plastic eggs** containing today's Bible verse. For each set, write the verse on six strips of paper, dividing the verse as follows: "This is my / body, which is / given for you. / Do this in /remembrance of me" / Luke 22:19.

Place individual strips in the plastic eggs. If possible, hide the sets of eggs on opposite sides of the room.

Say the verse and ask the students to repeat it with you. Divide the students into two teams. Tell each team which side of the room is theirs.

Say: When I say "Go!", run to your side of the room and find the six plastic eggs I have hidden for your team. Open the eggs to find the slips of paper inside. Work with your teammates to put the slips in the correct order to say today's Bible verse. The first team who has the verse in the correct order wins.

Supplies:
Reproducible 2E, cassette player

Zillies®:
Cassette

Sing

Give each student a copy of the words to the song "Amazing Grace" **(Reproducible 2E).** Ask everyone to follow along reading the words as you play the song on the **Cassette.** Play the song again and invite everyone to sing.

Supplies:
none

Zillies®:
none

Praise

Ask: Why is God's grace so amazing? (*God would give God's only Son to die for our sins. Because of Jesus' life, death, and resurrection, we are forgiven and have a new relationship with God.*)

Pray: Dear God, we thank you for your Son, Jesus. We thank you for the gift of Holy Communion that Jesus gave us. We still have that gift today. The bread and juice we have at Communion reminds us that Jesus gave his life for us and that Jesus is always with us. Amen.

Give each student a copy of HomeZone® to enjoy this week.

Memory Verse

This is my body, which is given for you. Do this in remembrance of me.

Luke 22:19

Pressed Flower Easter Bookmark

You will need tiny flowers that have been dried. To dry the flowers place them between folded sheets of typing paper. Place the paper inside the pages of a heavy book. Leave them in the book for several days.

Cut a bookmark from tagboard or heavy paper. Select a shape that reminds you of Easter, perhaps a cross. Carefully put a dab of glue behind each of the dried flowers and arrange them on the bookmark. Write an Easter message on the bookmark; for example, "Remember Jesus." When the glue has dried, cover the bookmark with clear adhesive plastic. Punch a hole in the top of the bookmark and tie a pretty ribbon through the hole.

Yummy Mayonnaise Muffins

You will need:
butter
2 cups self-rising flour
⅓ cup mayonnaise
1 cup milk

Preheat the oven to 450 degrees. Grease a muffin pan with butter. Mix the flour, mayonnaise, and milk in a bowl. Put one tablespoon of the batter in each greased muffin tin. Bake at 450 degrees for 10 to 12 minutes.

Make only half the recipe if you will be feeding four people or less.

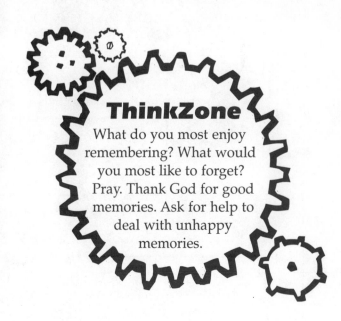

ThinkZone

What do you most enjoy remembering? What would you most like to forget? Pray. Thank God for good memories. Ask for help to deal with unhappy memories.

We remember Jesus and thank God for the new life Jesus brings.

Reproducible 2D

BibleZone®

Amazing Grace

Amazing grace! How sweet the sound
That saved a wretch like me!
I once was lost, but now am found,
Was blind but now I see.

Thru many dangers, toils and snares,
I have already come;
Tis grace has brought me safe thus far,
and grace will lead me home.

'Twas grace that taught my heart to fear,
and grace my fears relieved;
How precious did that grace appear
the hour I first believed.

Amazing! Amazing! Amazing! Oh, yeah!

When we've been there ten thousand years,
bright shining as the sun,
We've no less days to sing God's praise
than when we'd first begun.

Writers: Troy and Genie Nilsson
Publisher: Bridge Building Music
Copyright © 1995 Bridge Building Music/BMI
All Rights Reserved.
Used by permission of Brentwood-Benson Music Publishing, Inc.
From the Brentwood-Benson Music Publishing, Inc. recording *Hymns in the House*.

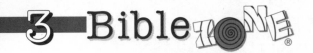

Road to the Cross

Enter the

Bible Verse
Truly this man was God's Son!
Matthew 27:54

Bible Story
Matthew 26:1-5, 14-16, 43-65; Mark 14:1-11, 43-65;
Luke 22:1-6, 39–23:49

After the Passover meal Jesus and his followers left the city and went to a garden on the Mount of Olives called Gethsemane. Obviously Jesus frequented this spot, because it was there Judas led the Temple guards to arrest Jesus. But why did the guards come to such an out-of-the-way place? Hadn't Jesus been teaching and healing all day at the Temple? Why did they not arrest him there? He was certainly more accessible at the Temple.

The answer is simple—popular opinion. The Pharisees and Sadducees had seen Jesus' celebrated entry into the city, and they were afraid to make a public spectacle of his arrest. But Passover was too volatile a time to let a dissident run loose in the city. Jesus was making inroads into their authority and was making them, the appointed leaders, look silly and unwise.

What motivated Judas to turn against his friend and teacher? The amount of money he received was barely enough to purchase a simple linen tunic. That was hardly enough to make a man betray a friend. Judas had seen what Jesus could do. Perhaps he hoped that if pushed, Jesus would reveal himself. Surely Jesus would drop his kind and forgiving attitude if it meant saving his own life. But Judas had not counted on God's motivation.

The Gospel writers do not exactly agree as to what happened that night. According to Matthew, Jesus had a hearing in front of the religious council. They accused him of blasphemy. But the council did not have the political authority to condemn a man to death. So they turned to the Roman governor, Pilate. Pilate, who hated the Jewish leaders, did not want to give in to their demands. Pilate tried to relieve himself of the responsibility for Jesus' fate. But he eventually gave in to the shouting crowd. Jesus was crucified. The question of who is responsible for Jesus' death is complex in even the simplest interpretation.

Choose one or more activities to immerse your children in the Bible story.

Zoom Into the Bible

Supplies:
Reproducible 3C,
Bible for each
student, scissors

Zillies®:
plastic eggs

(P) hotocopy and cut apart the question strips (**Reproducible 3C**). Cut the strips apart and place each strip in a **plastic egg.** Hide the eggs around the room.

Say: I have hidden plastic eggs around the room. Inside the eggs is information that will help us discover who killed Jesus. When you find an egg, open it and look for the answer for each question.

When all the eggs are open, have the students go in order of the verses to share their questions and answers.

Questions and Answers:

1. Read Luke 22:1-2. Who was looking for a way to put Jesus to death? *(priests and scribes)*
2. Read Luke 22:3-6. Who agreed to betray Jesus for money? *(Judas Iscariot)*
3. Read Luke 22:39. Where did Jesus go to pray? *(Mount of Olives)*
4. Read Luke 22:47-48. How did Judas betray Jesus? *(with a kiss)*
5. Read Luke 23:3. What was Jesus' answer when Pilate asked if Jesus was king of the Jews? *("You say so.")*
6. Read Luke 23:13-15. Did Pilate and Herod find a reason to kill Jesus? *(no)* What did they want to do to Jesus? *(have him flogged and released)*
7. Read Luke 23:18-19. Who did the crowd want released instead of Jesus? *(Barabbas)*
8. Read Luke 23:21. What did the crowds shout? *("Crucify him! Crucify him!")*
9. Read Luke 23:26. Who carried the cross for Jesus? *(Simon of Cyrene)*
10. Read Luke 23:42. What did one of the criminals who would die with Jesus want Jesus to do? *(remember him)*
11. Read Luke 23:44. What happened about noon? *(Darkness came over the whole land.)*
12. Read Luke 23:49. Who watched from a distance while Jesus died on the cross? *(the women who had followed him from Galilee)*

Enjoy the Story

Supplies:
Reproducibles 3A
and 3B

Zillies®:
none

(T) ell or read the story "The Holy Week Whodunit, Part 3" (**Reproducibles 3A and 3B**).

Ask: Who do you think killed Jesus?

37

The Holy Week Whodunit
(Part 3)

by Michael E. Williams

When the day of the debate came, Ms. Porter's room buzzed with excitement. The teacher had explained that, at different times, different groups had been blamed for Jesus' death. In the debate a group of students would act as defense attorneys for each of those groups. Brenda and May Lin would represent Pontius Pilate. Sean and Jasmine would defend the religious authorities. That meant Felix was left to defend the crowd by himself, but he promised that he would be serious about it.

"Is everyone ready for your presentations?" asked Ms. Porter.

"Ready!" came the voices of children from all three groups.

"When we left Jesus, he was ending his last supper with his disciples. They were going out to a garden called Gethsemane. Judas had turned Jesus over to the authorities for a payment of thirty pieces of silver. He came into the garden and pointed Jesus out to those who would arrest him by greeting him with a kiss. Even so, I think we decided that Judas should not bear the full blame for Jesus' death. There are three other possible suspects who will be put on trial today: the religious authorities, Pontius Pilate, and the crowd. Let's hear from the attorneys for the religious authorities first."

Jasmine began. "Jesus was a dangerous man to our clients. He had said some things that sounded like he put himself on a level with God, which would be blasphemy. For that the law required that he should die. Also, he had said some other things that made the Romans think that he was some kind of king or leader who would try to drive them out by force. When the Romans thought that about one Jewish person, it made it dangerous for all Jewish people. Something had to be done to stop this dangerous situation. Everything our clients did was within the law and was for the protection of all the people. That is why they are religious authorities in the first place, to protect the people who depend on them."

"But your clients were the ones who brought Jesus to our client in the first place," Brenda spoke up. She smiled at Ms. Porter, knowing that she was using the correct legal language and that her teacher would appreciate it.

Sean responded quickly. "Your client is the law, the Roman law. He was the only one who could do what needed to be done. The religious authorities had to go to Pilate because they really didn't have any authority, and he did."

"Why don't you present Pontius Pilate's case, Brenda?" Ms. Porter extended her hand to her student, who was already standing.

"Pontius Pilate did not usually stay in Jerusalem," Brenda began. "He liked to live in Caesarea Maritima, or Caesarea by the Sea. It was built by King Herod to be more Roman than a Roman city, so being a Roman, Pilate liked it there. He was only in Jerusalem for the Passover holiday."

"This does have something to do with his role in the death of Jesus, I suppose?" her teacher interrupted. Ms. Porter and the entire class knew that sometimes Brenda liked to show how much she knew about everything. Occasionally she would share her wealth of knowledge even when it didn't have anything to do with the topic they were discussing.

"It does," Brenda continued. "Often there was trouble during the Jewish holidays, and Pilate had to be in Jerusalem to take care of it. Our client was just doing his job. Whenever there was trouble, he was there to stop it. When Jesus was brought to him, our client asked him questions, and Jesus refused to give a straight answer. When Jesus was asked if he was a king, he told Pilate that he (Pilate, that is) had said so in the first place. Jesus said his kingdom was not of this world. Our client didn't know how to take these answers. Even though Jesus wouldn't really answer Pilate's questions, our client didn't think that Jesus was so dangerous, as the religious authorities said. He even tried to let Jesus go, but the crowds . . . ,"—at this point Brenda was staring at Felix, who was looking away and not really paying attention—". . . wouldn't let him. Pilate offered to let go either Jesus or Barabbas, and *THE CROWD* wanted Barabbas. We rest our case."

"Would you like to respond on behalf of the crowd, Felix?" Ms Porter asked.

Felix stood, looked at the other students, cleared his throat, and began. "How do we define crowd?" he said seriously. "A crowd is a group of people, I think we can all agree on that. But who is the crowd we are talking about here? Is it the crowd that shouted 'Hosanna' and waved palm branches? Or is it the crowd that shouted 'Crucify him!'? Are they the same crowd?"

"I'm confused. Who is he talking about?" Sean spoke up.

"Can you help us out a little, Felix? Who do you think the crowd is?" Ms. Porter inquired.

"I can, and I will. Just give me a minute. First let me tell you who the crowd is not. The crowd is not the women who were Jesus' followers, because they were crying there on the hill where he was crucified. Also, Jesus' male followers aren't a part of the crowd, since as soon as he was arrested, they made themselves scarce—except for Peter, who tells everybody he doesn't know who Jesus is.

"So the crowd might be the 'Hosanna!' and 'Crucify him!' crowds. And it might be the soldiers who nailed him to the cross and stood guard while he died. And it might be the soldiers who gambled for his cloak and made fun of him. And it might include the two thieves who were on crosses next to him on each side. And it might even include the religious authorities and Pontius Pilate. And it might even include you and me, since we probably would have done the same thing as the people then did.

"But it doesn't really matter who the crowd is, because Jesus looked at all of them (or us) and said, 'Father, forgive them, because they don't know what they are doing.' So if they are forgiven, they can't be guilty. End of case. Amen."

The room was silence for a moment as Felix sat down with an air of triumph. Then May Lin spoke up for the first time in this class. "It sounds like they, or we, were all guilty. All the suspects did it. Which is why, I guess, they, or we, all needed forgiveness."

Ms. Porter stood looking at the class in astonishment. "What a class!" was all she could say.

Reproducible 3B

1. Read Luke 22:1-2. Who was looking for a way to put Jesus to death?

2. Read Luke 22:3-6. Who agreed to betray Jesus for money?

3. Read Luke 22:39. Where did Jesus go to pray?

4. Read Luke 22:47-48. How did Judas betray Jesus?

5. Read Luke 23:3. What was Jesus' answer when Pilate asked if Jesus was king of the Jews?

6. Read Luke 23:13-15. Did Pilate and Herod find a reason to kill Jesus? What did they want to do to Jesus?

7. Read Luke 23:18-19. Who did the crowd want released instead of Jesus?

8. Read Luke 23:21. What did the crowds shout?

9. Read Luke 23:26. Who carried the cross for Jesus?

10. Read Luke 23:39. What did one of the criminals who would die with Jesus want Jesus to do?

11. Read Luke 23:44. What happened at about noon?

12. Read Luke 23:49. Who watched from a distance while Jesus died on the cross?

Reproducible 3C

BIBLEZONE®

Home Zone For Students

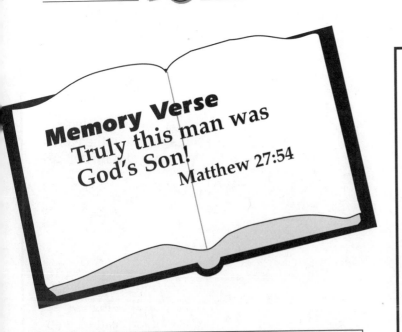

Memory Verse
Truly this man was God's Son!
Matthew 27:54

Pit Promises

Did you know that new life can come from a pit? All you need to do is save a pit from an avocado. Peel off the brown covering. Fill a small jar almost full of water. Stick three toothpicks into the pit and place the toothpicks over the edge of the jar so that the fat end of the pit is suspended over the water. Add water to the jar as the water evaporates. Soon the pit will send out roots, and eventually a green stem and leaves will grow! Then you can transplant your new plant into a pot of soil. Pinch back the plant to make it grown bushy and beautiful.

Mosaic Cookies

You will need:
1 (12-ounce) package semi-sweet chocolate chips
½ cup butter or margarine
1 (10½-ounce) package colored miniature
  marshmallows
1 cup chopped walnuts
3½ cups coconut

In the top of a double boiler, melt the chocolate chips and butter; stir to blend. Place marshmallows and nuts in a large mixing bowl. Pour the melted chocolate over the top of the marshmallows and nuts; stir carefully to coat. Chill about 15 minutes to make handling easier. Sprinkle the coconut on a bread board. Spoon ⅓ of the chocolate in a row about 10 to 12 inches long on top of the coconut. Carefully roll the chocolate in the coconut, shaping it to make a roll. Place on waxed paper or foil, wrap, and twist the ends. Repeat with the remaining mixture. Chill until firm. Slice to serve. Makes about 7 dozen cookies.

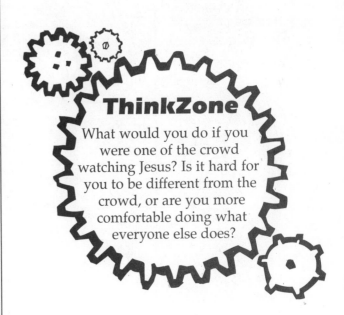

ThinkZone
What would you do if you were one of the crowd watching Jesus? Is it hard for you to be different from the crowd, or are you more comfortable doing what everyone else does?

Jesus gave his life so we can have new life.

43

Reproducible 3D

BibleZone®

In the Garden

I come to the garden alone,
While the dew is still on the roses.
And the voice I hear, falling on my ear,
the Son of God discloses.

As He walks with me, as He talks with me,
And He tells me I am His own.
And the joy we share as we tarry there,
none other has ever known.

He speaks and the sound of His voice
is so sweet the birds hush their singing,
And the melody that He gave to me,
within my heart is ringing.

As He walks with me, as He talks with me,
And He tells me I am His own,
And the joy we share, as we tarry there,
none other has ever known.

As He walks with me, as He talks with me,
And He tells me I am His own,
And the joy we share, as we tarry there,
none other has ever known.

Reproducible 3E

45

Jesus Lives!

Enter the

Bible Verse
He is not here, but has risen.

Luke 24:5

Bible Story
Matthew 28:1-10; Mark 16:1-8; Luke 24:1-35;
John 20:1, 11-18; 21:3-19

The story of Jesus' resurrection is the heart and soul of the Christian faith: Jesus IS alive! Because Jesus lives, we have the new life God promised.

Justice in Bible times was swift and without appeal. Jesus was crucified on the same day he was tried and condemned—Friday. The priests had heard the rumors of Jesus' claim to rise from the dead on the third day. So they stationed guards around Jesus' tomb. They also had the tomb sealed so that the disciples could not sneak inside and steal the body, and then claim that Jesus had risen. The Jewish sabbath began on that same Friday at sunset and continued through sunset on Saturday. During that time no work could be done, including preparing a body for proper burial. So on the morning after the sabbath, some of Jesus' women friends came to the tomb to give the body a proper burial with oils and spices.

The grieving women were not prepared for the reality that greeted them. When the women arrived at the tomb, it was empty. Between the message of the angel and the meetings with Jesus himself, the company of believers who had followed Jesus came to the wonderful realization that Jesus was indeed alive.

Easter is the highlight of the Christian year, a day of great celebration! Jesus is alive! Today is a time to celebrate new life in all its forms. Your students may, at Easter, have questions about the resurrection. Answer them as simply and as honestly as possible. As adults we still don't have all the answers. It's perfectly acceptable to say, "I don't know." What we do know is that with God, anything is possible.

Create a celebratory mood in your class. The Easter story, while it is the basis for our Christian faith, is harder to tell than the Christmas story. A cross and an empty tomb are not as warm and fuzzy an image as a stable filled with farm animals. But we want your students to understand that God gave Jesus new life and that, through Jesus, we also have new life.

Jesus gives new life.

Scope the ZONE

ZONE	TIME	SUPPLIES	⊚ ZILLIES
Zoom Into the Zone			
Get in the Zone	5 minutes	pages 173 and 174, cassette player	Cassette
Rock 'n Roll	10 minutes	shoebox lids or poster-board, felt-tip markers	bouncing rock balls or ping pong balls
BibleZone®			
Zoom Into the Bible	20 minutes	Bible for each student	none
Enjoy the Story	15 minutes	Reproducibles 4A and 4B	none
LifeZone			
Beautiful Butterflies	15 minutes	Reproducible 4C, different-colored tissue paper, scissors, markers, pencils, white glue	none
Ping Pong Play	10 minutes	Reproducible 4C, old panti-hose, wire coat hangers, scissors	ping pong ball, yarn
Sing	5 minutes	Reproducible 4E, cassette player	Cassette
Praise Pipeline	10 minutes	construction paper, paper clips	ping pong balls

⊚ Zillies® are found in the **BibleZone® FUNspirational® Kit.**

47

Zoom Into the

Choose one or more activities to catch your children's interest.

Supplies:
pages 173 and 174, cassette player

Zillies®:
Cassette

Supplies:
shoebox lids or posterboard, felt-tip markers

Zillies®:
bouncing rock balls or ping pong balls

Cardboard
tissue paper squares

Get in the Zone

Have "The Bible Zone" **(Cassette)** playing as the students arrive. **Say: Welcome to the BibleZone!** If you have any new students, take time to make introductions and to tell them what your class experienced last week. Give out nametags if necessary **(page 173).**

Give each student a copy of "The Bible Zone" **(page 174)** and invite everyone to sing along with you.

Rock 'n Roll ✓

Divide the students into pairs. Give each pair a shoebox lid (or piece of posterboard approximately the same size). In the center of the lid (or posterboard), have them draw a circle with a felt-tip marker, about three inches in diameter, and color it in. Then give each team a **bouncing rock ball** or a **ping pong ball.**

Say: Today's Bible story tells about the time when Jesus' friends came to the garden to give his body a proper burial. They were expecting to find the tomb all sealed up by the authorities. In fact, they even wondered how they were going to get in. But when they got there, something exciting had happened. The stone had been rolled away, and their friend Jesus wasn't there. God had raised him from the dead. Let's play a game where we try to roll the stone into the doorway of the tomb. The circle in the center of the box lid or posterboard is the opening to the tomb.

When you give the signal to begin, the two students must hold on to either ends of their lids or pieces of posterboard. Then, without touching the rock ball or ping pong ball, they must try to roll it until it is sitting totally in the opening of the tomb. Play until all the students have had a chance to get their balls onto the circle.

Ask: How did you get your "rock" to move without touching it? (*jiggled the box lid, tilted it up or down*) **Was it easy to move it where you wanted it?** (*no*) **Could you move a very large rock this way?** (*no*)

Say: God provided a miracle. The rock had been moved. The tomb was empty. Jesus was alive!

48

Choose one or more activities to immerse your children in the Bible story.

Zoom Into the Bible

Supplies:
Bible for each student

Zillies®:
none

(B)e certain each student has a Bible. Divide the class into six teams. **Say: The four Gospels all tell us what happened at the Resurrection, when God brought Jesus to life again.**

Ask Team One to read Matthew 28:1-10.
Ask Team Two to read Mark 16:1-8.
Ask Team Three to read Luke 24:1-12.
Ask Team Four to read Luke 24:13-35.
Ask Team Five to read John 20:1, 11-18.
Ask Team Six to read John 21:3-19.

Invite the teams to share the stories they read. **Ask Teams One, Two, Three, and Five: Who was in the story?**
(*Matthew: Mary Magdalene, the other Mary, and the angel*)
(*Mark: Mary Magdalene; Mary, the mother of James; Salome; young man in a white robe*)
(*Luke: Mary Magdalene; Mary, the mother of James; Joanna; other women; two men in dazzling clothes*)
(*John: Mary Magdalene; Jesus appeared to Mary Magdalene*)
Ask: What was the common element in the stories? (*the empty tomb*)

Ask Teams Four and Six: Who saw Jesus?
(*Luke: two disciples*)
(*John: disciples—Simon Peter, Thomas, Nathanael, sons of Zebedee [James and John], two others*)

Enjoy the Story

Supplies:
Reproducibles 4A and 4B

Zillies®:
none

(T)ell or read the story "The Holy Week Whodunit, Part 4" **(Reproducibles 4A and 4B).**

Ask: Who do you think killed Jesus?
Why does that question not matter anymore?
What is is the new question for us to think about?

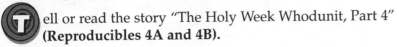

Jesus gives new life.

The Holy Week Whodunit
(Part 4)

by Michael E. Williams

Everyone was in the classroom, except Ms. Porter. It was very strange since she was never late. She was usually there before anyone else, waiting when the students arrived. Where could she be today?

"What will we do if Ms. Porter doesn't come?" asked Jasmine.

"We can't leave," Brenda answered. "Our parents are in their classes."

"We could spend our time making a get-well card for Ms. Porter," May Lin offered.

"We don't know that she's sick," Sean spoke up.

"Or," it was Felix this time, "we could find the stairs that lead to the bell tower. I'll bet there's a ghost up there."

About the time Felix had made this last suggestion, the door to the classroom opened. In walked a woman who looked a lot like Ms. Porter. She was dressed in a long, light-blue dress that reached almost to the sandals that she wore on her feet. There was a white cloth covering her hair. She looked just like a woman out of one of the illustrations from their student Bible.

"Hello," she said.

A few hesitant "Hi's" escaped from the students' lips. They stared at the visitor, not really sure if she was a stranger or just Ms. Porter in costume.

"My name is Mary, and I come from Magdala. I am a follower of Jesus. You have been learning what happened to him during the last week of his life. You have been trying to solve a mystery: Who killed Jesus? We tried that too, just after his death. It was easy to blame this one or that one. We could have picked each other apart blaming one another. What we discovered was that there was a deeper mystery, a more important question that we hadn't even realized then. But I'm getting ahead of myself.

"You see, I thought that Jesus was dead. In fact, I had seen him die. I had helped with the burial preparations. His body was placed in one of the rooms of a new tomb that belonged to a very wealthy man in town. Usually his body would have stayed there until all the flesh was gone. Then his bones would have been collected and placed in an ossuary, a box designed to hold the bones of the dead.

"I returned to the tomb on the first day of the week, the day you call Sunday. I expected to find the body just as we had left it when the Sabbath had come upon us too soon. But there was no body there. It was gone. I was terribly upset. I had heard stories of graves being robbed, and I was afraid that was what had happened here. Or perhaps some of Jesus' other followers had taken his body somewhere for safekeeping.

"I turned and saw a man I did not recognize right away. I thought he might be the caretaker of the tombs. I told him that I had come to find the man who had been

Reproducible 4A

BibleZone®

laid in the tomb. Then he looked at me and said, 'Mary.'

"I knew that voice. I had heard it thousands of times. It was the voice of Jesus. But I knew it couldn't be. I had seen him die. Yet, now I heard his voice calling my name. 'Rabboni, Teacher,' I said to him. And I reached out for him. It seemed like the natural thing to do.

"'Don't try to touch me just yet,' he told me. 'Go and tell my other disciples that I am going ahead of them to Galilee. I will meet them there.' So I did.

"I heard many reports of others seeing Jesus after that. Peter told me that they had fished all night and saw someone standing on the shore. Like me, they didn't recognize who it was at first. He told them to fish out of the other side of the boat. They thought he was crazy, but when they tried it, they could not get the nets in because they were so heavy with fish.

"Peter knew it was Jesus then, he told me. When he got to shore, he ate with Jesus; they all did. Then Jesus asked Peter three times if he loved him. Each time Peter told him that he did. Each time his feelings were more hurt that Jesus had to ask again. Each time Jesus told him, 'Feed my sheep. Feed my lambs. Feed my sheep.'

"Later Peter told me that Jesus may have asked him if Peter loved him three times because Peter had denied knowing him three times. One kind of evened the other out. One question for each denial, to wipe each one away. After the third question the slate was clean again.

"Some of his other followers told of walking from Jerusalem to Emmaus. They met a stranger on the way and began talking to him. He seemed to know nothing about

what had happened to Jesus. So these two followers told the stranger all that had happened during the few days before that. They told how Jesus had been tried and then crucified and buried. They even mentioned that some of his followers had said that they had seen him alive after that.

"When they arrived at Emmaus, the two invited the stranger in to eat with them. When he broke the bread, they recognized that the stranger they had been talking to had been Jesus all along. Then they looked again, and he was gone.

"So that is what I have come to tell you. There are those of us who can tell you that Jesus is alive. So the mystery about who is responsible for his death doesn't matter anymore. There is no more blaming. There is no point to it. How can you convict someone of a death when the victim is alive? So the mystery you have been seeking to solve is really no mystery at all. Goodbye."

The stranger, who by now everyone knew was Ms. Porter in costume, got up and started to leave.

"Wait a minute," May Lin stopped her. "You said that there was another question, a more important one. What is it?"

"You're right. I did say that. We found that once the question of who to blame was out of the way, we were able to hear the real question. It is the one followers of Jesus have been struggling with ever since. That is: *What does it take to be a disciple of Jesus?*"

With that the visitor turned and left the room.

As she went, she and the class heard Felix exclaim, "What a teacher!"

51

Reproducible 4B

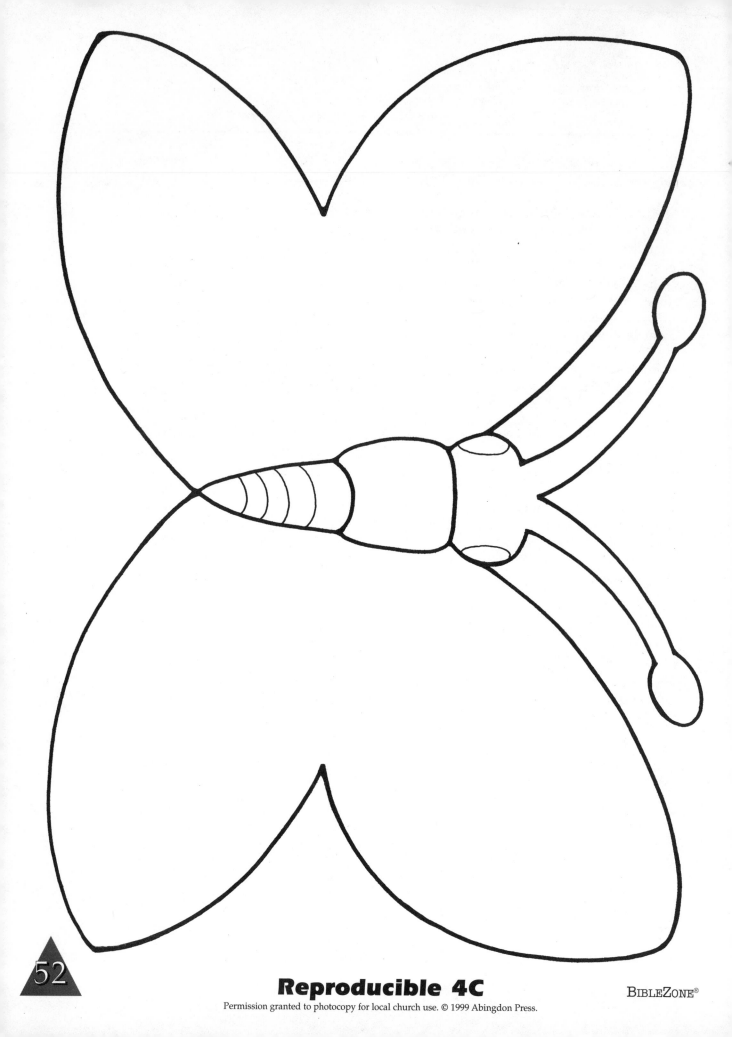

52

Reproducible 4C

Permission granted to photocopy for local church use. © 1999 Abingdon Press.

Beautiful Butterflies

Give each student a copy of the butterfly pattern **(Reproducible 4C)**. Have precut one-inch squares of different-colored tissue paper. Also have markers, pencils, and white glue available.

Say: **Color the body of the butterfly using markers. Then wrap one square of tissue on the eraser end of a pencil, add a tiny drop of glue on the top of the tissue, and press it onto the wings of the butterfly. Continue until you have completely covered the wings.**

Say: **At Easter we celebrate Jesus' resurrection from the dead. One of the symbols of Easter is the butterfly. Why do you think butterflies remind Christians of Easter?**

Explain that the chrysalis that a caterpillar forms reminds many Christians of the tomb. The caterpillar appears to have died and then is born again into a beautiful butterfly.

Say: **This process reminds us of the resurrection of Jesus. Jesus was killed, but God raised him from death to life. The symbolism of the butterfly also helps us to understand why the followers did not recognize Jesus at first after the Resurrection. The butterfly does not resemble its old caterpillar self!**

Supplies:
Reproducible 4C, different-colored tissue paper, scissors, markers, pencils, white glue

Zillies®:
none

Ping Pong Play

Show the students how to make racquets by using old pantihose and wire coat hangers. Bend the hangers to make a diamond shape. Cut the leg from the pantihose, slip the leg over the hanger, and tie it at both ends. Bend the handle of the hanger closed or wrap **yarn** around it.

Divide the class into two teams. Have the teams stand facing one another. Say today's Bible verse: "He is not here, but has risen" (Luke 24:5). Display the verse **(Reproducible 4D)** where everyone can see it.

Say: **Use your racquets to bat the ping pong ball back and forth between the teams, down the line. As the ball comes to you, say the next word of the Bible verse.**

Continue play up and down the lines several times.

Supplies:
Reproducible 4C, old pantihose, wire coat hangers, scissors

Zillies®:
ping pong ball, yarn

Supplies:
Reproducible 4E,
cassette player

Zillies®:
Cassette

Sing

Give each student a copy of the words to the song "And This Is Eternal Life" **(Reproducible 4E).** Play the song on the **Cassette** and ask the students to follow along. Play the song again and invite them to sing.

Ask: What is eternal life? How do we have eternal life? Why is that possible?

Supplies:
construction paper, paper clips

Zillies®:
ping pong balls

Praise Pipeline

Have each student make a paper tube out of rolled construction paper. Have him or her secure both ends of the tube with a paper clip.

Divide the class into two teams. Have each team line up side by side with paper tubes in hand. Have the first person in line put a **ping pong ball** in his or her tube; then have a relay race to see which team can pass the ping pong ball through all the tubes on their team. Caution the students that no hands must touch the ball except the first person on the team.

Say: Each time the ping pong ball enters your tube, call out one sign of new life! *(Give examples if necessary—butterflies, flowers blooming, babies, green grass, spring following winter)*

When the game is over, repeat the signs of new life. **Pray: Dear God, we thank you for all the signs of new life. We thank you for your Son, Jesus, who died and rose to live again to give us new life. Amen.**

Jesus gives new life.

Give each student a copy of HomeZone® to enjoy this week.

Memory Verse

He is not here, but has risen.

Luke 24:5

Butterfly Buns

You will need:
¼ cup butter, melted
¼ cup sugar
½ teaspoon cinnamon
1 can prepared biscuits (found in the dairy section of the grocery)
¼ cup confectioner's sugar
1 tablespoon milk

In a glass measuring cup, melt the butter in the microwave oven. In a small bowl, mix together the cinnamon and the sugar.

Separate the biscuits. Cut in half. Dip each half in the melted butter and then roll in the sugar. Then place on the baking sheet, curved sides together, touching. Bend the edges out to represent butterfly wings.

Bake as directed on the can. Remove from the oven. Drizzle the mixture of confectioner's sugar and milk over the wings as icing. Serve for Easter brunch.

Butterfly Garden

Christians often associate the butterfly with the death and resurrection of Jesus Christ. Because this creature begins life as a caterpillar and then miraculously changes into a butterfly, we use this metaphor to help us understand Jesus' transformation from man to Christ. Everyone loves to have these beautiful creatures visit our yards and gardens during the summer. Whether your family lives in an apartment in the city, a house in the suburbs, or a farm in the country, you can plan a garden that will invite these creatures to visit in great numbers. Some of the plants need a large space; others can grow in a pot on a window ledge or in a flower box. Butterflies are attracted to fragrant flowers and flowers that have clusters of blooms. Try some of these: yarrow or Queen Anne's lace, heliotrope, viburnum, bee balm, lilac, pansies, nasturtiums, cosmos, foxglove, sweet William, or lupine. Morning glories, sweet peas, and purple wisteria also provide shelter for your butterfly visitors.

ThinkZone
Every year the coming of Spring reminds us that Jesus brings the gift of new life. What changes have you seen this spring in the world around you? in yourself?

Jesus gives new life.

He is not here, but has risen.

Luke 24:5

56

Reproducible 4D

BIBLEZONE®

And This Is Eternal Life

And this is eternal life that they may know Thee,
The only True God and Jesus Christ, (*Clap four times.*)
Whom Thou hast sent.
This is eternal life that they may know Thee,
The only True God and Jesus Christ, (*Clap 4 times.*)
Whom Thou hast sent.

And this is eternal life that they may know Thee,
The only True God and Jesus Christ, (*Clap four times.*)
Whom Thou hast sent.
This is eternal life that they may know Thee,
The only True God and Jesus Christ, (*Clap four times.*)
Whom Thou hast sent.
Whom Thou hast sent.

(sung at the same time as the above stanza)
Hallelujah, Hallelujah.
Hallelujah, Hallelujah!
Hallelujah, Hallelujah.
Hallelujah, Hallelujah!
Hallelujah!

Writer: Steve Jones
Copyright © 1986 New Spring Publishing/ASCAP
All Rights Reserved.
Used by permission of Brentwood-Benson Music Publishing, Inc.
From the Brentwood-Benson Music Publishing, Inc. recording *Kids Sing Praise, vol. 1.*

Reproducible 4E

Do You Believe?

Enter the ZONE®

Bible Verse
Blessed are those who have not seen and yet have come to believe.

John 20:29

Bible Story
John 20:19-31

The women were the first to know of Jesus' resurrection. When they announced that not only was Jesus gone from the tomb, but also that they had seen him and touched him, the apostles thought this was just an idle tale. But this was just the first of the many appearances and visions that the whole company experienced.

On the evening of that first day of the week, the disciples were gathered together behind locked doors. Due to the events of the past few days, they were terrified that what had happened to their teacher and friend could just as easily happen to them. Suddenly Jesus appeared in their midst. Those who experienced this visitation were filled with wonder and were eager to share the event with those who had not been there.

But there was one who, no matter how many times the others told him about Jesus' appearance, would not believe until he had actually seen and touched Jesus for himself. One week later, when the disciples had gathered together, Jesus again came to them. This time Thomas was present. Jesus told

Thomas to touch the wounds that he had received upon the cross. Only then would Thomas believe that it was truly Jesus.

How often do we use the expression "seeing is believing" when referring to a seemingly impossible event? We rely on our senses to validate what we perceive to be true.

Older elementary boys and girls need to verbalize experiences and questions about God, Jesus, and their faith.

So how do you teach someone about God? God cannot be seen or felt or touched or tasted or heard. And what about Jesus? We only have the stories that someone else wrote about him to inform us of who he was and what he did. The rest of the story must be accepted by the students on the basis of faith.

Sharing your faith helps boys and girls understand that some things cannot be perceived in concrete terms, and also helps them understand how others can accept these things and believe in them.

We can believe in Jesus, who brings new life.

Scope the

ZONE	TIME	SUPPLIES	⊚ ZILLIES
Zoom Into the Zone			
Get in the Zone	5 minutes	page 174, cassette player	Cassette
Seeing Is Believing	10 minutes	8½-inch squares of paper, water	none
BibleZone®			
Zoom Into the Bible	15 minutes	Bible for each student	none
Enjoy the Story	15 minutes	Reproducibles 5A and 5B	none
LifeZone			
Believe It or Not!	10 minutes	none	atom balls
Dig Deep	10 minutes	Reproducible 5D, markers or crayons	none
Sing	5 minutes	Reproducible 5E, cassette player	Cassette
Believer's Buttons	5 minutes	Reproducible 5C, scissors, tape	none
I Believe!	10 minutes	none	celestial ball

⊚ Zillies® are found in the **BibleZone® FUNspirational® Kit.**

Zoom Into the ~~ZONE~~

Choose one or more activities to catch your children's interest.

Supplies:
page 174,
cassette player

Zillies®:
Cassette

Supplies:
8½-inch squares
of paper, water

Zillies®:
none

Get in the Zone

Welcome the students and let them know how happy you are to see them. Have "The Bible Zone" **(Cassette)** playing and invite the students to sing with you. Have copies of the words **(page 174)** available.

Seeing Is Believing

Give each student an 8½-inch square of paper. **Say: I'm feeling very thirsty. You all look thirsty too. Let me pour you a drink of water. Hold out your papers.**

Go around the group and begin to pour water (just a few drops) on one of the student's papers. (The water will run off.)

Ask: Doesn't this sound like a good idea? Why not? (*The paper won't hold a cup of water.*) **Don't you think you can drink from your piece of paper? Who believes you can? Who doesn't believe?**

Say: Actually, you can drink from this paper. All you need to do is make a few folds. But I can tell that you have to see it before you will believe it.

Show the students how to fold the paper into a paper cup in this way:

Step 1: Fold the square in half along the diagonal, forming a triangle. Hold the triangle so that it makes an arrow pointing upward. The folded edge will be on the bottom.
Step 2. Fold point B upward so that it touches the middle of the left edge (AC). Fold point C upward so that it touches the middle of the right edge (AB).
Step 3. Fold the front point (A) into the pocket formed when you folded the right side over. Then fold the back point into the central pocket. To open the cup, push in from both sides.

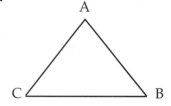

Pour a little water into each student's cup and let each take a drink.

Say: Sometimes we have to see something for ourselves before we will believe it. One of Jesus' disciples, Thomas, would not believe before he could see.

Choose one or more activities to immerse your children in the Bible story.

Zoom Into the Bible

 ay: Jesus had died and had risen from the grave. We know that Jesus appeared to his followers. Our Bible story today tells us about one of the disciples who did not believe.

Be certain each student has a Bible. Ask everyone to read John 20:19-31. Ask:

1. **What did Jesus say to the disciples?** *("Peace be with you.")*
2. **What did Jesus show them?** *(his hands and his side)*
3. **How did the disciples react to seeing Jesus?** *(They were happy; they rejoiced.)*
4. **Who was not with the disciples at that time?** *(Thomas)*
5. **What did Thomas say he would have to do to believe?** *(see the mark of the nails in Jesus' hands, put his finger in that mark, and put his hand in Jesus' side)*
6. **What was Thomas referring to?** *(the wounds Jesus suffered on the cross—the nails through his hands and the sword through his side)*
7. **A week later Jesus joined the disciples when Thomas was there. What happened?** *(Jesus told Thomas to touch his wounds.)*
8. **Did Thomas recognize Jesus?** *(Yes.)*
9. **What did Jesus say to Thomas?** *("Blessed are those who have not seen and yet have come to believe.")*

Supplies:
Bible for each student

Zillies®:
none

Enjoy the Story

ell or read the story "The Holy Week Whodunit, Part 5" (Reproducibles 5A and 5B).

Ask: How would you feel if you saw someone who had died?
Do you think Thomas was Doubting Thomas or Brave Thomas?
What can we do to show others that we have Jesus' spirit?

Supplies:
Reproducibles 5A and 5B

Zillies®:
none

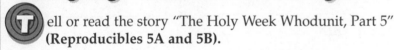

We can believe in Jesus, who brings new life.

The Holy Week Whodunit
(Part 5)

by Michael E. Williams

The question that Ms. Porter, the visiting stranger who was really their teacher, had asked at the end of the last class stayed with the class members. "What does it take to be a disciple of Jesus?" She had said that it was the most important question, more important than who had killed Jesus. They were left wondering what the next class session would be like.

This week Ms. Porter was waiting in the classroom when the students arrived. When they were all there, she said, "I'm sorry I couldn't be with you last week. I hope you all learned a lot from your substitute." There was only a hint of a smile at the corners of her mouth.

All her students smiled back and nodded.

"As we move on toward Holy Week today, we will look at one more story from the Bible. Your teacher from last week, Mary Magdalene, told me that you decided that who killed Jesus might not be the real question here. Instead, what it takes for you to be his disciple is the real mystery for you to solve. So, the question is not, 'How did he die?' but 'How do we live?' Right?"

Again there were nods around the room.

"Let's see if this story might help us solve that mystery." Ms. Porter opened her Bible and read them a story. In it the disciples of Jesus were in hiding. They were afraid that what had happened to Jesus might happen to them. One day Jesus came to them in their hiding place. Of the ones who were left, only Thomas, who was called the Twin, was missing.

Jesus appeared to his disciples, breathed on them, said, "Peace" to them, then let them see his wounds from the crucifixion.

When Thomas returned, the others were excited. "We've seen the Lord. We've seen the Lord," they kept saying. Finally Thomas said, "I'll believe it when I see it." Then he added, "I'll believe it when I get to touch his wounds."

A week later Jesus came back, and this time Thomas was there. He showed the wounds on his hands and feet and side to Thomas and told him that he could touch them, if he wanted. Instead, Thomas fell on his knees and said, "My Lord and my God."

Jesus didn't punish Thomas for not believing his friends when they told him about Jesus' visit. He simply told Thomas that he was blessed because he had seen and believed, and that there will be other disciples who wouldn't have the chance to see Jesus, but who would believe anyway. They would be blessed too.

When she was finished reading the story, Ms. Porter asked, "What can we learn from this story about being a disciple?"

"We shouldn't doubt Jesus," Brenda spoke up.

"Thomas didn't doubt Jesus; he doubted the other disciples," Sean responded.

"Do you ever doubt what your friends tell you?" their teacher asked.

"All the time." Brenda looked at Sean as she answered.

Reproducible 5A

BibleZone®

"Do you think you would believe it if they told you that someone who had died had come back to visit them?" Ms. Porter probed.

"I don't think so." This time it was Sean's turn to look at Brenda.

"So we can say that Thomas was honest with his friends and with Jesus," Ms. Porter said.

"Maybe he thought they were so afraid that they were seeing things?" Felix offered.

"And Jesus never said he was wrong to doubt them," Jasmine said. "After all, they had gotten to see Jesus the first time, and Thomas hadn't."

"So disciples of Jesus are honest about what they have experienced, even with their friends," their teacher summed up.

"Where was Thomas the first time Jesus came?" May Lin asked.

"The Bible doesn't say where he was," Ms. Porter answered. "Where do you think he might have been?"

"Maybe he went out to the grocery store," Jasmine suggested.

"Or maybe he went out jogging," Felix piped up.

"If all the rest of the disciples were hiding because they were afraid, does that mean that Thomas wasn't hiding?" Jasmine asked earnestly. "Does that mean he wasn't afraid?"

"So instead of Doubting Thomas we could call him Brave Thomas," Sean observed.

"Can we say that one of the things you can say about disciples of Jesus is that they are brave?" the teacher asked.

"But all the rest were afraid," Brenda observed.

Sean spoke up again. "Maybe Thomas was afraid too. He just did what he had to do anyway. So disciples of Jesus may be afraid, but they do what they have to do anyway."

"Maybe that's what it is to be truly brave," Ms. Porter added.

"Why did Jesus breathe on them?" Brenda questioned. "That seems kind of strange."

"Maybe he was trying out a new breath mint?" It was Felix, of course.

Ms. Porter ignored Felix's answer. "It does not come through in English, but the same word in Greek means breath, wind, and spirit. So when he breathed on his disciples, he was giving them his spirit."

"So Jesus' disciples are people who have Jesus' spirit," May Lin spoke up.

"What does it take to be a disciple of Jesus?" Ms. Porter asked the class.

"To have Jesus' spirit," May Lin answered.

"To be brave even when we are afraid," Sean responded.

"To be honest with everybody," Jasmine added.

Ms. Porter smiled. "I think we may have solved our Holy Week mystery. You have a lot to think about during this Holy Week. You've given me a lot to think about too. We will all have a more meaningful Holy Week and Easter for the work we've done. Thank you."

I'm a
Believer!

I'm a
Believer!

I'm a
Believer!

I'm a
Believer!

I'm a
Believer!

I'm a
Believer!

I'm a
Believer!

I'm a
Believer!

I'm a
Believer!

I'm a
Believer!

I'm a
Believer!

I'm a
Believer!

I'm a
Believer!

I'm a
Believer!

I'm a
Believer!

I'm a
Believer!

I'm a
Believer!

I'm a
Believer!

I'm a
Believer!

I'm a
Believer!

Reproducible 5C

BibleZone®

Choose one or more activities to bring the Bible to life.

Believe It or Not!

Supplies:
none

Zillies®:
atom balls

(S) ay: Let's play a game of believers versus non-believers.

Select one student to be the non-believer. Have everyone else, the believers, stand in a circle fairly close together, facing in. Hold up an **atom ball.**

Say: I will give an atom ball to one believer. You must pass the atom ball from believer to believer. If the non-believer tags you while you have the atom ball in your hands, you become the non-believer! Also, if you drop the atom ball, you automatically become the non-believer! You can pass the ball from believer to believer, or you can toss it across the circle.

If you have a large group, use two atom balls and have two non-believers outside the circle. To create an extra challenge use only one-handed throws and catches.

Dig Deep

Supplies:
Reproducible 5D, markers or crayons

Zillies®:
none

(G) ive each student a copy of today's Bible verse **(Reproducible 5D).** Invite everyone to add color to the drawing.

Say: Dig deep into your thoughts before you answer this: What do you think it would have been like to have seen Jesus after the crucifixion?

Ask everyone to say today's verse with you: "Blessed are those who have not seen and yet have come to believe"(John 20:29).

Sing

Supplies:
Reproducible 5E, cassette player

Zillies®:
Cassette

(G) ive each student a copy of the words to the song "Joyful, Joyful" **(Reproducible 5E).** Play the song on the **Cassette** and ask everyone to follow along. Play the song again and invite everyone to sing with you.

Choose one or more activities to bring the Bible to life.

Believer's Buttons

Say: Sometimes it is hard to believe the things we cannot see, taste, touch, or feel. We have never actually seen or touched Jesus, but we know that he lived, died, and lives again.

Give each student a strip of believer's buttons **(Reproducible 5C). Say: For us to be followers of Jesus, we must share the good news of Jesus with others. Wear one of the buttons. Today find three other people to give a button to. Tell those people why you believe in Jesus.**

I Believe!

Say: I believe that Jesus loves me. (*Toss the celestial ball to one of the students.*)

Ask: What do you believe?

Go around the group, letting the students say what they believe about Jesus. When everyone has had a chance to contribute, sign the words, "Don't doubt; believe" together.

Pray: Dear God, we believe that Jesus is your Son. We believe that Jesus is the Messiah. We believe that Jesus loves us always. We believe that Jesus gives us new life. Amen.

 We can believe in Jesus, who brings new life.

Give each student a copy of HomeZone® to enjoy this week.

Home Zone For Students

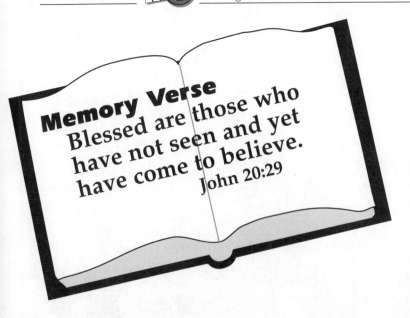

Memory Verse
Blessed are those who have not seen and yet have come to believe.
John 20:29

Wet or Dry?

You will need:
¾ cup cornstarch
½ cup water
glass bowl
spoon

Use a spoon to evenly blend the water with the cornstarch in the bowl. You can see for yourself that water is going into the mixture. When it is all mixed up, form a ball by rolling it between your palms. Is it wet or dry?

It looks wet, but it doesn't feel wet!

Do not wash the mixture down a drain. Dispose of the mixture in the trash or in the compost bin.

Impossible Candy

Can you make candy from a potato? Yes!

You will need:
one small potato
confectioner's sugar
peanut butter

Peel and cut up a small potato. Put it in a pan and cover the potato with water. Cook on the stove until it is easy to stick a fork into the potato. Drain the water and mash the potato.

Add confectioner's sugar to the potato until the dough is stiff. Sprinkle confectioner's sugar on wax paper and roll the dough out.

Spread peanut butter over the dough. Begin on one side and roll the dough into a log. Wrap the log in cellophane paper and chill in the refrigerator. Cut the log into small pieces to serve.

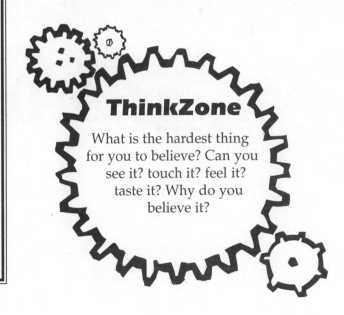

ThinkZone

What is the hardest thing for you to believe? Can you see it? touch it? feel it? taste it? Why do you believe it?

We can believe in Jesus, who brings new life.

67

Blessed are those who have not seen

and yet have come to believe.

John 20:29

Reproducible 5D

BibleZone®

Joyful, Joyful

Joyful, joyful, we adore Thee,
God of glory, Lord of love;
Hearts unfold like flowers before Thee,
Opening to the sun above.
Melt the clouds of sin and sadness,
Drive the dark of doubt away;
Giver of immortal gladness,
Fill us with the light of day.

Thou are giving, and forgiving,
ever blessing, ever blessed,
Well-spring of the joy of living,
Ocean depth of happy rest!
Thou our Father, Christ, our Brother—
All who live in love are Thine;
Teach us how to love each other,
Lift us to the joy divine.

Joyful, joyful, joyful, joyful, joyful, joyful, joyful, joyful.

Mortals, join the mighty chorus
Which the morning stars began;
Father love is reigning o'er us,
Brother love binds man to man.
Ever singing, march we onward,
Victors in the midst of strife,
Joyful music leads us sunward
in the triumph song of life.

Joyful, joyful, joyful, joyful, joyful, joyful, joyful, joyful,
Joyful, joyful, joyful, joyful, joyful, joyful, joyful, joyful,
Joyful, joyful, joyful, joyful, joyful, joyful, joyful, joyful.

Text by Henry Van Dyke; Music by Ludwig Van Beethoven
Arrangement by Troy and Genie Nilsson
Copyright © 1995 New Spring Publishing/ASCAP
All Rights Reserved.
Used by permission of Brentwood-Benson Music Publishing, Inc.
From the Brentwood-Benson Music Publishing, Inc. recording *Hymns In the House*.

Reproducible 5E

69

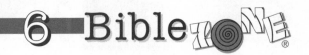

In the Beginning

Enter the

Bible Verse
O LORD, our Sovereign,
how majestic is your name in all the earth!
Psalm 8:1

Bible Story
Genesis 1:1-13

The Book of Genesis is a proclamation that God is the source of all Creation. It is a statement of faith that answers important questions for God's people. Although the Book of Genesis does not offer scientific explanations for how the world came to be, it does answer far more important questions about why God created and who we are in relationship to God. The Greek word *genesis* means "beginning." The Hebrews' stories told of God who was present at the beginning of the cosmos and upon whom all living things depended for their being. From these stories the people learned that nothing is independent, self-created, or self-sustaining. God is the source of all that exists.

The images of the story describe Creation in the language of the Hebrews. For these early people, the earth was the center of the universe. They thought the earth was flat, with a domed sky. In the sky there were windows to let the waters through. As we read the story, we can experience the world as these people experienced it.

Retelling the Hebrew creation stories is important for Christians of all ages. The stories help us to see the world with new awe and wonder. The story of Creation in the Book of Genesis affirms our beliefs about God as Creator and challenges us to reaffirm the part God calls us to play in the story.

Surely the Hebrew people would be amazed by the vast scientific knowledge we have of the universe today. But none of that scientific knowledge changes the wonder of God's creating. In fact the more we learn about the complexity of nature, the vastness of the universe, or the abilities of human beings, the more we marvel at the miracle of God's creation.

Some students may ask, "Who made God?" According to the Bible, God simply was. God is. God always will be. Because creation is a gift to all of us from God, caring for all that God created is not something we can choose to do; it is something God commands us to do.

God is the source of all Creation.

Scope the

ZONE	TIME	SUPPLIES	⊚ ZILLIES®
Zoom Into the Zone			
Get in the Zone	5 minutes	page 174, cassette player	Cassette
Chaos Hats	10 minutes	Reproducible 6D, newspapers, glue, feathers, nature magazines, wrapping paper	none
Chaos Colors	10 minutes	black, white, blue, brown, and green construction paper; scissors, masking tape	none
BibleZone®			
Zoom Into the Bible	20 minutes	Bible for each student; black, white, blue, brown, and green construction paper; scissors	none
Enjoy the Story	15 minutes	Reproducibles 6A and 6B	none
LifeZone			
Breath Tests	10 minutes	none	paper blow-outs, ping pong balls
Totally Terrific Terrariums	15 minutes	Reproducible 6C, wide-mouth quart jars with lids, sand, small gravel, charcoal chips, dead leaves or peat moss, soil, small wild plants, spray bottles with water, and large spoons	none
Sing	5 minutes	Reproducible 6E, cassette player	Cassette
Bible Verse Blast	10 minutes	Reproducible 6B (bottom)	atom ball
Pray	5 minutes	none	none

⊚ Zillies® are found in the **BibleZone® FUNspirational® Kit.**

71

Zoom Into the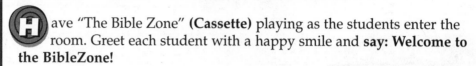

Choose one or more activities to catch your children's interest.

Supplies:
page 174,
cassette player

Zillies®:
Cassette

Get in the Zone

Have "The Bible Zone" **(Cassette)** playing as the students enter the room. Greet each student with a happy smile and **say: Welcome to the BibleZone!**

Give each student a copy of the words to "The Bible Zone" **(page 174).** Play the song again and invite everyone to sing with you.

Supplies:
Reproducible 6D,
newspapers, glue,
feathers, nature
magazines,
colorful wrapping
paper

Zillies®:
none

Chaos Hats

Ask: Can you create something out of nothing? *(Accept answers.)*

Place a stack of newspapers on the table. **Say: These newspapers are not anything special. Let's see what we can create.**

Give each student a copy of the diagram showing how to fold a hat **(Reproducible 6D).** Show the students step by step how to fold their hats.

Say: God created everything from nothing. God is the source of all Creation. In the beginning there was only God.

Supplies:
black, white, blue,
brown, and green
construction
paper; scissors,
masking tape

Zillies®:
none

Chaos Colors

Cut large squares of black, white, blue, brown, and green construction paper. Divide the students into two teams, and have the teams stand on opposite sides of the room. Give each team one-half of the squares. Use masking tape to mark a line down the center between the two teams.

Say: When I say "Go!" begin tossing the squares over to the other team's side. When I say "Stop!", we will see which team has the most squares. The winner is the team with the fewest squares!

When the game is over, **say: All those colors being thrown around was chaos. In the beginning, before God's creation, there was only chaos. There was no order or shape. There was no purpose. God gave everything shape and purpose.** (Save the squares to use again.)

Choose one or more activities to immerse your children in the Bible story.

Zoom Into the Bible

Be certain each student has a Bible. Ask the students to look at the table of contents in their Bibles. **Ask:**

How many testaments are in the Bible? *(two)*
What are they? *(Old Testament and New Testament)*
What is the name of the first book in the Old Testament? *(Genesis)*

Say: The first book in the Old Testament is the Book of Genesis. Genesis gets its name from a Greek word that means "beginning." The book not only is the beginning of the Bible, but it also tells about the beginning of creation.

Ask everyone to find Genesis and read Genesis 1:1-13. **Ask:**
Who was there at the beginning when the world was created? *(God)*
What was the first thing God called into being? *(light)*
What did God call the light? *(day)*
What did God call the darkness? *(night)*
What did God call the dome that was created? *(sky)*
What did God call the dry land? *(earth)*
What did God call the waters that had been gathered together? *(seas)*
What did God tell the earth to put forth? *(vegetation: seeds and plants)*
How did God feel about the creation? *(It was good.)*

Place the pile of squares of black, white, blue, brown, and green construction paper where everyone can reach them. **Say: Choose a partner. Read verses 1-13 again. Work with your partner to take one square of each color and put the colors in the order of creation. You will have to decide what the colors mean to you.**

When all the pairs have their colors in order, ask them to explain the colors they choose to represent the order of creation.

Supplies:
Bible for each student; black, white, blue, brown, and green construction paper; scissors

Zillies®:
none

Enjoy the Story

Tell or read the story "Before" (Reproducibles 6A and 6B). Ask:
What do you think chaos was like before God created?
Why do you suppose God decided to create?
Why do you think God chose the order of creation that God used?
What do think God is like?
Why do you suppose God thought creation was good?

Supplies:
Reproducibles 6A and 6B

Zillies®:

Before

by Michael E. Williams

In the beginning there was the slow, steady breathing of God. It was the first sound, the first song sung before anything else ever was. God's breathing was the rhythm of life before there was life, the breath of the world before there was a world. That breath was the wind blowing across the waters when there was nothing but water. The dark waters rippled with the rhythm of the divine breath, and there was no one there to see it but the one who breathed the first breath. In the beginning there was God.

That breath was God's spirit traveling through the darkness, across the waters toward the future before anyone but God dreamed there was a future. God's spirit was a living thing, a creative thing. Everything we know and love about the world was made through that spirit, carried into being on that breath. Before that, though, there was God.

Then there was a word carried on the breath. The word was "let." Then another followed fast upon it. That word was "light." Then with an explosion of breath the word "be" came roaring out of God's mouth. "Let light be." And these were the first words, the first speech. Before there were words, and before there was speech, there was the speaker. That speaker was God.

The words poured out across the waters in streams of light, the first light of the first morning before the sun or moon were even a vague inkling. God was the light, and the fire of God's voice was its brightness. God saw the light standing next to the darkness, and the darkness side by side with the light, and it was wonderful.

When the light was in place, God called it a day.

The God blew a bubble that became a dome. There were waters above the bubble and waters below. The waters above the bubble God called sky, and the waves in that sky God called clouds. The waters below the bubble were called sea, and the waves were just called waves. It was the wind of God's breath that moved the clouds around the sky and the waves across the sea. The breath of God's spirit moved across the waters once again. God looked from the waters to the waters, and it was wonderful.

When the waters were in place, God called it a day.

Then the voice of God called the earth forth. The dry land came out of the waters like a baby's face turning to its mother's voice. Everywhere on the land there were hills and valleys, mountains and meadows. Wherever the voice of God traveled, there was beauty. Trees stood tall and shrubs squatted beside them. Buds burst forth and flowers colored the earth with reds and blues, purples and yellows. The fruit trees were weighed down with pears and persimmons, with apples both delicious and crab. God saw the beauty of the flowers and the trees as they dressed the earth, and it was truly wonderful.

Reproducible 6A

When the earth and trees, the shrubs and flowers, were in place, God called it a day.

Before!
Before there was earth, there was God.

Before!
Before there were trees and shrubs, there was God.

Before!
Before there were flowers and fruit, there was God.

Before!
Before there was earth, there was God.

Before!
Before there was sky and sea, there was God.

Before!
Before there was light, there was God.

Before!
Before there was wind, there was God's breath, God's creative spirit making all that is from the nothing that was.

Before!
God!

O Lord, our Sovereign, how majestic is your name in all the earth!
Psalm 8:1

Reproducible 6B

Totally Terrific Terrariums

You will need
- ➡ a wide-mouth quart jar with a lid
- ➡ small gravel
- ➡ sand
- ➡ charcoal chips
- ➡ dead leaves or peat moss
- ➡ soil
- ➡ small wild plants
- ➡ a spray bottle with water
- ➡ a large spoon

Use the spoon to make layers of materials in the jar. Cover the bottom of the jar with gravel. Cover the gravel with sand. Then add the charcoal chips and dead leaves or peat moss. Put about two inches of soil on top.

Plant the wild plants in the soil. Spray a little water in the terrarium.

Keep the terrarium in a cool spot with very little light for two days. After two days use a paper towel to carefully wipe out all the water that has collected on the inside of the jar.

Move the terrarium to a place where it will receive indirect sunlight.

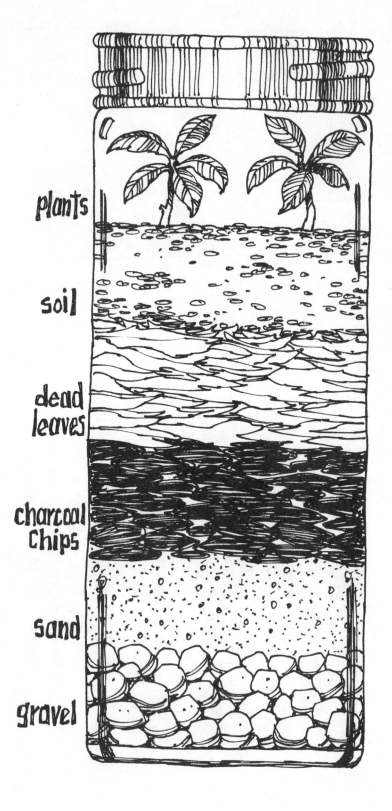

plants

soil

dead leaves

charcoal chips

sand

gravel

76

Reproducible 6C

BIBLEZONE®

Choose one or more activities to bring the Bible to life.

Breath Tests

Supplies:
none

Zillies®:
paper blow-outs, ping pong balls

(H)ave the students line up at one end of the room. Ask them to get on their hands and knees. Give each student a **paper blow-out** and a **ping pong ball**.

Say: When I say "Go," put the ping pong ball on the floor in front of you. Begin blowing into the paper blow-out to move your ping pong ball across the floor to the other side of the room. The first person to reach the other side of the room first wins. You may only use your breath to move the ball. You cannot touch it with any part of your body or with the paper blow-out.

For a greater challenge have the students race to one side of the room and back.

Say: The story "Before" describes God's breath as the breath of the world before there was a world. What do you suppose God's breath, God's spirit, is like? What power do you think is in God's breath?

Totally Terrific Terrariums

Supplies:
Reproducible 6C, wide-mouth quart jars with lids, small gravel, sand, charcoal chips, dead leaves or peat moss, soil, small wild plants, spray bottles with water, and large spoons

Zillies®:
none

(A)sk the students to select partners. (If you have a large class, you may need to divide the students into teams of three.) Provide the following supplies for the teams to share: wide-mouth quart jars with lids, small gravel, sand, charcoal chips, dead leaves or peat moss, soil, small wild plants, spray bottles with water, and large spoons.

Give each team a copy of the directions for making terrariums (**Reproducible 6C**) and invite them to begin. While they work, talk about creation. Remind the students of the order of God's creation.

Ask: Why do you suppose God created so many kinds of plants? What do plants need to live? Why do you think God planned for plants to need soil, light, and water? What do you think the earth would be like without plants?

Choose one or more activities to bring the Bible to life.

Supplies:
Reproducible 6E,
cassette player

Zillies®:
Cassette

Sing

Give each student a copy of the words to the song "In the Beginning" **(Reproducible 6E).** Play the song on the **Cassette** and ask everyone to follow along. Play the song again and invite everyone to sing the refrain with you.

Supplies:
Reproducible 6B
(bottom)

Zillies®:
atom ball

Bible Verse Blast

Ask everyone to stand in a close circle. Display today's Bible verse **(Reproducible 6B, bottom)** where everyone can see it. Ask the students to repeat it with you: "O LORD, our Sovereign, how majestic is your name in all the earth!" (Psalm 8:1).

Say: I will bounce the atom ball in the middle of the circle. The person who catches it must say the first word of the Bible verse and bounce the ball again. The person who catches it then says the second word of the verse and bounces the ball again. Keep going until we have said all the words of the Bible verse.

When the entire verse has been said, have the students repeat the game over and over, each time saying the verse faster.

Supplies:
none

Zillies®:
none

Pray

Ask the students to share their prayer concerns. Write them down as each one is mentioned.

Pray: Dear Creator God, you are our Sovereign. You have created all we know and see. You have created all we do not know and have not seen. You are our awesome God, who planned every part of creation perfectly. We ask that you hear our concerns. (*Name them.*) We know that you will be with us and the people we have named always. Amen.

 God is the source of all Creation.

Give each student a copy of HomeZone® to enjoy this week.

Memory Verse
O LORD, our Sovereign, how majestic is your name in all the earth!
Psalm 8:1

Go Play in the Mud!!!

Think about God's creation. Select something you want to mold to show part of Creation. To do this, you can play in the mud—clean mud.

You will need Ivory soap shavings from a bar of Ivory soap, toilet paper, and water.

Shred the toilet paper into a bowl and mix with the Ivory soap shavings. Add small amounts of water until the mixture is the right consistency for you to make your creation about Creation!

Earthquake Cake

You will need:
1 cup chopped pecans
1 cup shredded coconut
1 (18.25 ounces) box German chocolate cake mix
1 (16-ounce) box powdered sugar
1 (8-ounce) package cream cheese, softened
1 stick margarine, softened

Combine the pecans and coconut and sprinkle in the bottom of a greased 9-by-13-inch pan. Mix the cake batter according to package directions. Pour the cake batter over the pecans and coconut. Cream together the cream cheese, margarine, and powdered sugar. Pour over the cake batter. (Do not stir into the cake batter.) Bake at 350 degrees for 45 minutes. The top of the cake will crack and be lumpy as if an earthquake had struck!

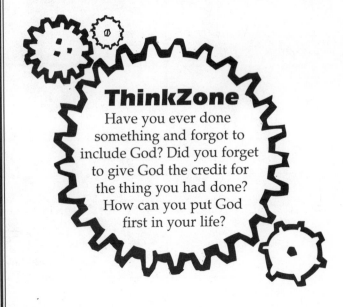

ThinkZone
Have you ever done something and forgot to include God? Did you forget to give God the credit for the thing you had done? How can you put God first in your life?

ZONE IN: God is the source of all Creation.

Chaos Hats

You will need a sheet of newspaper (two pages with a fold down the middle).

Fold the outer edges down so they make a point at the top center.

Fold the bottom flap up to meet the edge of the triangle. Fold it over again, and do the same thing on the other side.

Roll up the front brim, and you've got yourself a cool hat!

If you want to decorate your hat, glue on feathers, magazine pictures showing creation, or small fans folded from colorful wrapping paper.

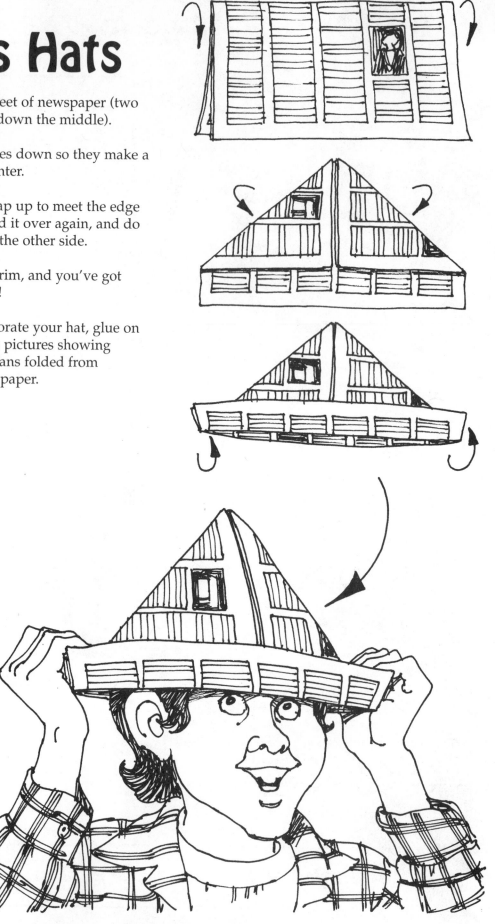

80

Reproducible 6D

BibleZone®

In the Beginning

Genesis 1:1, the fun's just begun in Genesis 1:1.
Genesis 1:1, the fun's just begun in Genesis 1:1 . . . (*Repeat.*)

In the beginning, God created the heavens and the earth
In the beginning, God created the heavens and the earth . . .
(*Repeat.*)

Day 1 . . . Let there be light
Day 2 . . . God made the sky
Day 3 . . . Plants, land, and sea
Day 4 . . . Sun, moon, and stars
Day 5 . . . Fish and the birds
Day 6 . . . Animals and man
Day 7 . . . was the day He blessed
He said, "I did good! I'll take a rest!"

In the beginning, God created the heavens and the earth
In the beginning, God created the heavens and the earth . . .
(*Repeat.*)

It is done, check it out, you're gonna love it
It is good, so have fun and take care of it

Genesis 1:1, the fun's just begun in Genesis 1:1
Genesis 1:1, the fun's just begun in Genesis 1:1 . . .

In the beginning, God created the heavens and the earth
In the beginning, God created the heavens and the earth . . .
(*Repeat.*)

In the beginning, God created the heavens and the earth
In the beginning, God created the heavens and the earth.

Words and music by Troy and Genie Nilsson.
Copyright © 1997 Bridge Building Music/BMI.
All rights reserved.
Used by permission of Brentwood-Benson Music Publishing, Inc.
From the Brentwood Music Publishing, Inc. recording, *Scripture Rock*.

Reproducible 6E

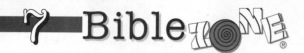

Sun, Moon, Stars

Enter the

Bible Verse
The heavens are telling the glory of God;
and the firmament proclaims his handiwork.

Psalm 19:1

Bible Story
Genesis 1:14-19

When God spoke, there was Creation. God separated light from darkness, and there was day and night. Then God separated the waters, and there was sky and earth. God brought forth dry land from the seas. Finally, God set in place the sun, the moon, the stars, and the galaxies of the universe.

The poetic account of Creation in the Bible shows that the ancient Hebrews had little knowledge of the true nature of the universe as we know it today. To them the earth was the center of the universe. While they might have been aware of the phases of the moon, they knew nothing of the planets that orbit the sun. They did not know that the sun was just another medium-sized star in a galaxy of many stars. How overwhelmed they would have been to hear about the billions upon billions of galaxies that exist beyond our own. Even scientists today are awed by the vastness.

But people then recognized the orderliness of creation, as do people now. God had a plan for it all.

As you read Genesis, think about its purpose. It is not an eyewitness account. It is not instruction in history or geography. Clearly it is the reflection of people who are considering great human questions: Where do we come from? How did creation begin? Why does creation continue?

In these Scriptures we discover what humankind has believed for thousands of years. God is the center of this finely tuned world. God provides everything necessary for life and for the organization of life.

God created the sun, moon, and stars.

Scope the

ZONE	TIME	SUPPLIES	⊚ ZILLIES®
Zoom Into the Zone			
Get in the Zone	5 minutes	page 174, cassette player	Cassette
Blindfold Bloopers	10 minutes	four blindfolds	none
BibleZone®			
Zoom Into the Bible	15 minutes	Bible for each student	none
Enjoy the Story	15 minutes	Reproducibles 7A and 7B	none
Celestial Chase	10 minutes	none	inflatable celestial ball
LifeZone			
Celestial Creations	15 minutes	Reproducible 7D, black construction paper, black bed sheet, tape	night sky stickers
Celestial Chairs	10 minutes	Reproducible 7C, scissors, chairs, tape, cassette player	Cassette
Sing	5 minutes	Reproducible 7E, cassette player	Cassette
Sign 'n Praise	10 minutes	none	none

⊚ Zillies® are found in the **BibleZone® FUNspirational® Kit.**

Zoom Into the Zone

Choose one or more activities to catch your children's interest.

Supplies:
page 174,
cassette player

Zillies®:
Cassette

Get in the Zone

Have "The Bible Zone" **(Cassette)** playing as the students enter the room. Greet each student with a happy smile and **say: Welcome to the BibleZone!**

Give each student a copy of the words to "The Bible Zone" **(page 174).** Play the song again and invite everyone to sing with you.

Supplies:
four blindfolds

Zillies®:
none

Blindfold Bloopers

Divide the students into four teams and ask each team to stand in a different corner of the room. Have one blindfold ready for each team to use.

Say: We are going to pretend it is night and very dark, and we have work to do. Each team should have one person put on a blindfold. When I say "Go," the person wearing the blindfold should do the task I request. No one can touch the persons wearing the blindfolds, but teammates can talk and say clues that help. The first player to finish the task gets a point. Then we will get a new player for each team and a new task. We will see which teams gets the most points.

Begin by giving simple tasks, such as "Take off your shoes and put them by the door." Keep score to see which players finish first. Play until each student has had a turn. Try to make each task a little more difficult. Some tasks you may want to suggest are: Find a paper towel on the table and wipe a window clean. Find one piece of trash on the table or floor and put it in the trash can. Find a Bible and put it on the table. Write your name on a piece of paper and give it to me.

After everyone has played, **ask: Was it difficult to work in the dark? Why? Why do you suppose God created nighttime? Why do you suppose God created daytime? What did God create to help us see during the day?** *(sun)* **What did God create to help us see at night?** *(moon, stars)*

 God created the sun, moon, and stars.

Choose one or more activities to immerse your children in the Bible story.

Zoom Into the Bible

Be sure each student has a Bible. Ask everyone to read Genesis 1:14-19. Say: **The Bible says God created two great lights.**

Ask: **What do we call the one that rules the day?** (*sun*)
What do we call the one that rules the night? (*moon*)
How did God feel about creation? (*It was good.*)

Supplies:
Bible for each student

Zillies®:
none

Enjoy the Story

Tell or read the story "The Argument" (**Reproducibles 7A and 7B**). Ask:
What is most important to you—the sun, moon, or stars? Why?
What is most important to other people you know—the sun, moon, or stars? Why?
What makes something important to God? (*Anything created by God is important to God.*)
If something is important to God, is it also important to us? How?

Supplies:
Reproducibles 7A and 7B

Zillies®:
none

Celestial Chase

Say: **Do you know what a light year is?** (*Accept answers.*) **A light year is the distance light travels in one year. Light travels about 186,000 miles a second, so a light year is about 6 trillion miles. One very bright star in the sky is Sirius, which is 8.7 light years away! Rigel, another very bright star, is 1,400 light years away! God's creation IS awesome!**

Ask everyone to wander around the room. Give one student the **inflatable celestial ball**. Say: **Whoever gets tagged with the ball must say today's Bible verse from Psalm 19:1: "The heavens are telling the glory of God; and the firmament proclaims his handiwork." You then get the celestial ball and try to tag someone else.**

After several students have been tagged and have said the verse, ask everyone to say it together. **Ask: What is God's handiwork?**

Supplies:
none

Zillies®:
inflatable celestial ball

85

The Argument

by Michael E. Williams

One day the Sun, Moon, and Stars had a disagreement. Each one claimed that it was more important than the others. Since they could never settle the matter on their own, they asked some of the other creatures to help them determine which was the most important.

The lion said, "Sun is the most important, because the Sun rules over the sky like I rule over the jungle. Sun is more powerful."

The owl had a different point of view. "Moon is greater, because when I am out hunting at night, I depend on the Moon to be a landmark for me in the sky. Moon is more necessary."

Turtle expressed still a third opinion. "The Stars are pinpricks of light that decorate the blanket of night. They are the dancers that who continually circle the sky to a music only they can hear. Stars are more beautiful."

Others began to toss about their own, sometimes negative, thoughts.

"The Sun is too hot," said the polar bear.

"The Moon is too dim," said the mole.

"The Stars are too small," said the elephant.

So the argument continued until Sun, Moon, and Stars decided to take the matter to a higher court. The three went together to plead their case before the seat of the greatest judge of all, God.

The Creator of the universe heard their bickering and asked what the problem was. They all spoke at once, interrupting each other so that God could not understand any of them.

Finally, God called for quiet. "Each of you tell me what you think the problem is." Since it has always been a good idea to do what God asks you to do, the three settled down.

Sun began. "Your Godliness, these two creatures claim to be my equal. Yet I am the brightest light in the sky. Even you called me 'The Greater Light to Rule the Day.' Without me there would be no food growing in the fields for people to eat. There would be no warmth to take away the chill of night. The world would be a cold, dark place if it were not for me.

"So, I submit that the Sun, my very self, is the greatest of all the lights of the sky, perhaps the greatest thing in all your creation."

The Sun beamed, very proud of the case he had presented on his behalf.

The Moon spoke next. "Our Creator, Sun has spoken well, and much that he has said is true. He is important during the day, but what about at night? Who shines then?

"I believe you will find that the Moon rules the night, just as the Sun rules the day. People mark their months by my changing face. And I am a creature of many disguises. At one time I am a sliver almost too slender to see. At another I'm a bowl ready to hold the grapes for your dinner. On occasion I'm a shiny silver coin high in the sky. Then another time I am a large yellow round of butter hanging just above the horizon. I am ever changing but ever there as a beacon in the night sky. How can I be a lesser light?"

In silence God pondered the testimony of Sun and Moon, then looked toward the Stars to see what they had to say.

Stars spoke. "Have you ever imagined a blank, black night sky with nothing to punctuate its darkness but the moon? That is exactly what you would see when you looked up at night if it were not for the Stars.

"People stare skyward and see pictures in my patterns. Some imagine a bull, a goat, twins, a water carrier. The sky and I are the canvas on which the artistic yearnings of your creatures are projected.

"And think about the traffic on your seas, if sailors had no Stars to steer their ships by. How would they navigate the unmapped oceans without my help?

"Also, what would the children of the world make wishes on if there were no Stars? So, you see, O Gracious One, Stars are by far the most important of the lights of the sky."

God listened and pondered all that had been said. "What is it to be important? To be powerful can make you feel important. To be necessary can make you feel important. To be beautiful can make you feel important. But what is it to truly be important?

"Sun, you are powerful, but that is not why I love you. You are my beloved child, my creation. I made you and called you good. That is why you are important to me, and if you are important to me, then you're important.

"Moon, you are necessary, but that is not why I love you. You, too, are my beloved child, my creation. I made you and called you good. That is why you are important to me, and if you are important to me, then you're important.

"Stars, you are beautiful, but that is not why you are important. You, too, are my beloved child, my creation. I made you and called you good. That is why you are important to me, and if you are important to me, then you're important.

"You are all a part of my family along with the rest of creation. You are all my beloved children, and none of you is more important than the other. I have given each of you gifts to share with all my creation, and each gift is important.

"So, Sun, share your gift of light. You are precious to me beyond measure.

"Moon, share your gift of light. You are precious to me beyond measure.

"Stars, share your gift of light. You are precious to me beyond measure.

"And you who are listening to this story, don't be concerned that someone else seems to be more important than you are. They are not. You are all my beloved children. Just share your gift of light. You are precious to me beyond measure."

Reproducible 7B

Reproducible 7C

BibleZone®

Celestial Creations

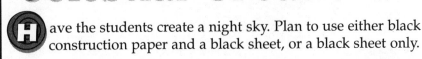

Have the students create a night sky. Plan to use either black construction paper and a black sheet, or a black sheet only.

Say: God created a wondrous night sky filled with millions of stars. In comparison to how many there are, we only know a few of the stars.

Tape together a few sheets of black construction paper. Give each student a copy of the star patterns **(Reproducible 7D)**. Invite everyone to work together to use the **night sky stickers** to create constellations on the paper. When finished, tape the paper to the underside of a large table and drape a sheet over the table. If you will be using the sheet only, have the students place stickers on the sides of the sheet. Drape the sheet over a table with the stickers on the inside. Let the students lie on the floor with their heads under the sheet to observe the night sky they created.

Supplies:
Reproducible 7D, black construction paper, black bed sheet, tape

Zillies®:
night sky stickers

Celestial Chairs

Make enough copies of the sun, moon, and star pictures **(Reproducible 7C)** so that each student will have a picture. Arrange the chairs in a circle. Randomly attach one picture to each chair with a piece of tape. Leave space between each chair so that the students can get around them without bumping into one another.

Say: God created the sun, the moon, and the stars. They are all a part of God's great plan for creation. As I play music, each of you will march around the circle behind the chairs. When the music stops, hold onto the back of the chair in front of you. I will say, "God created . . ." and name either the sun, the moon, or the stars. If you are standing behind the item I mention, you must change places with another person who is standing behind that item somewhere else in the circle. You must do this before I count to five. If you are standing behind one of the other items, you simply take your seat. Whoever does not get to a chair before I count to five must come to the middle of the universe, and we will remove his or her chair.

Continue play until most of the chairs have been removed from the circle.

Supplies:
Reproducible 7C, scissors, chairs, tape, cassette player

Zillies®:
Cassette

89

Choose one or more activities to bring the Bible to life.

Supplies:
Reproducible 7E,
cassette player

Zillies®:
Cassette

Supplies:
none

Zillies®:
none

Sing

(G)ive each student a copy of the words to the song "In the Beginning" **(Reproducible 7E).** Play the song on the **Cassette** and ask everyone to follow along. Play the song again and invite everyone to sing the refrain with you.

Sign 'n Praise

(S)ay: **When God created the sun, moon, and stars, God saw that it was good.**

Teach everyone how to sign the phrase, "And God saw that it was good."

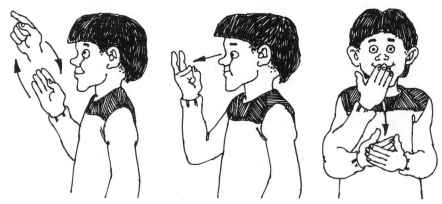

Lead the students in the following litany:
In the beginning, before there was anything else,
There was darkness, and there was God.
Then God created light.
(*Sign "And God saw that it was good."*)
Now there was darkness, called Night,
And there was light, called Day.
(*Sign "And God saw that it was good."*)
And God created two great lights,
The sun to rule the Day, and the moon to rule the Night.
(*Sign "And God saw that it was good."*)
Now there was Night, and there was Day.
Now there were sun and moon and stars.
(*Sign "And God saw that it was good."*)

Give each student a copy of HomeZone® to enjoy this week.

Sun Cooking

The sun is a very important part of God's creation. Not only does it provide light and warmth to the earth, but it can also be used to provide energy for cooking and for doing other things. Experiment with using sunlight for cooking. You will need these items: round bottom thin plastic bowl or paper bowl, aluminum foil, twist tie, clear plastic wrap, drinking straw, marshmallow, and towel.

Line the bowl with aluminum foil. Smooth out the wrinkles and fold the foil over the edges so that it hugs the sides. Skewer the marshmallow with the straw. Cut the straw so that it will rest about halfway down inside the bowl. Set the straw in the bowl so that the marshmallow doesn't touch the foil. Cover the bowl with clear plastic. Secure with a twist tie beneath the bowl. Set the bowl facing the sun so that the sun lights the entire inside. Use a towel to prop up the bowl. Check every fifteen to thirty minutes. When the marshmallow feels very soft, it is ready to eat.

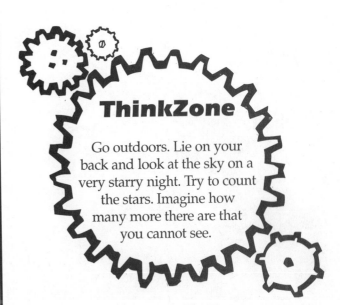

ThinkZone

Go outdoors. Lie on your back and look at the sky on a very starry night. Try to count the stars. Imagine how many more there are that you cannot see.

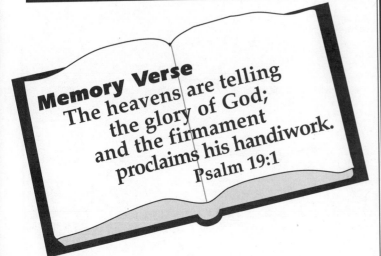

Memory Verse

The heavens are telling the glory of God; and the firmament proclaims his handiwork.

Psalm 19:1

Moon Balls

You will need:
2 cups dry milk
2 cups raisins
3½ cups graham cracker crumbs
1⅓ cups honey
2 cups peanut butter

Combine 2 cups dry milk, 2 cups raisins, and 3 cups graham cracker crumbs. Add 1⅓ cups honey and 2 cups peanut butter. Mix well.

Roll the mixture into small balls.

Place ½ cup graham cracker crumbs in a large plastic bag. Place several balls in the bag at a time and shake them to coat them. Place the balls on a cookie sheet. Refrigerate to chill. Enjoy eating moon balls!

God created the sun, moon, and stars.

91

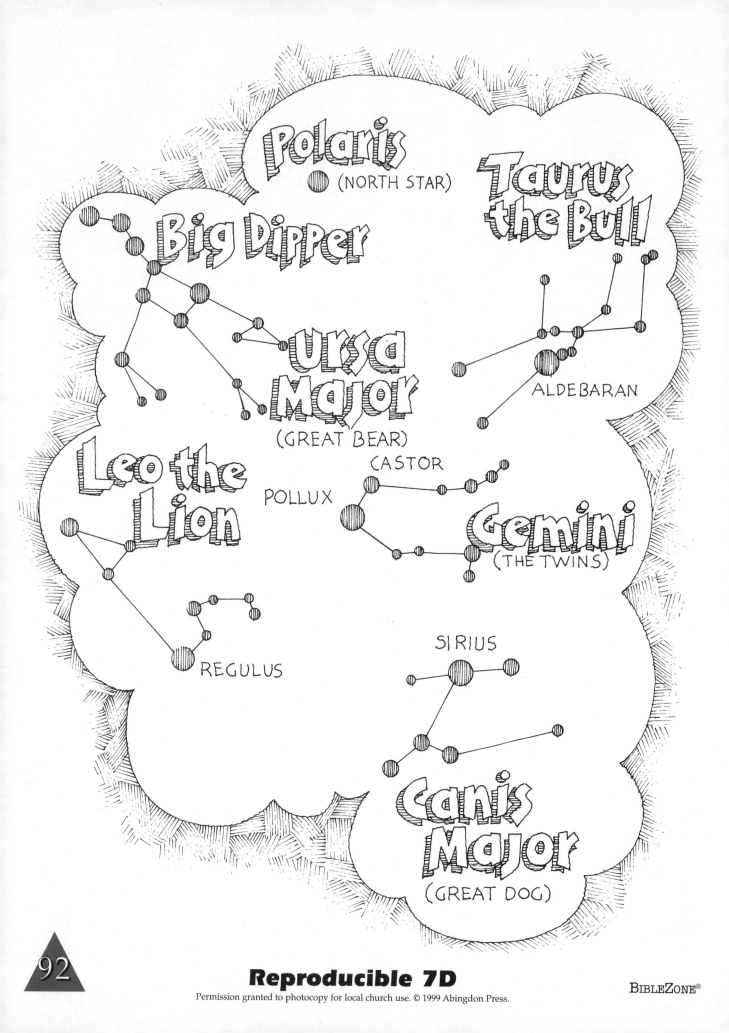

Polaris (NORTH STAR)

Taurus the Bull

Big Dipper

Ursa Major (GREAT BEAR)

ALDEBARAN

Leo the Lion

CASTOR

POLLUX

Gemini (THE TWINS)

REGULUS

SIRIUS

Canis Major (GREAT DOG)

Reproducible 7D

BibleZone®

In the Beginning

Genesis 1:1, the fun's just begun in Genesis 1:1.
Genesis 1:1, the fun's just begun in Genesis 1:1 . . . (*Repeat.*)

In the beginning, God created the heavens and the earth
In the beginning, God created the heavens and the earth . . .
(*Repeat.*)

Day 1 . . . Let there be light
Day 2 . . . God made the sky
Day 3 . . . Plants, land, and sea
Day 4 . . . Sun, moon, and stars
Day 5 . . . Fish and the birds
Day 6 . . . Animals and man
Day 7 . . . was the day He blessed
He said, "I did good! I'll take a rest!"

In the beginning, God created the heavens and the earth
In the beginning, God created the heavens and the earth . . .
(*Repeat.*)

It is done, check it out, you're gonna love it
It is good, so have fun and take care of it

Genesis 1:1, the fun's just begun in Genesis 1:1
Genesis 1:1, the fun's just begun in Genesis 1:1 . . .

In the beginning, God created the heavens and the earth
In the beginning, God created the heavens and the earth . . .
(Repeat.)

In the beginning, God created the heavens and the earth
In the beginning, God created the heavens and the earth.

Words and music by Troy and Genie Nilsson.
Copyright © 1997 Bridge Building Music/BMI.
All rights reserved.
Used by permission of Brentwood-Benson Music Publishing, Inc.
From the Brentwood Music Publishing, Inc. recording *Scripture Rock*.

Reproducible 7E

93

All God's Creatures

Enter the ZONE

Bible Verse

LORD, you have made so many things!
How wisely you made them all!
The earth is filled with your creatures.
Psalm 104:24, *Good News Bible*

Bible Story
Genesis 1:20-25

There was land and sea and sky. There were plants in abundance. There were warmth and light; day and night; and the seasons, as God prepared the earth for a more sophisticated form of life. God then made living creatures of many kinds. First God filled the waters with fish and other water-dwelling creatures. Then God filled the air above the earth with birds. Finally, God brought forth creatures of infinite diversity to walk upon the land.

God created animals to share the earth with the plants and, eventually, with human beings. There were animals to provide food, clothing, building materials, and transportation. There were animals that played their part in the balance of all of nature. And there were animals that would provide comfort and companionship for human beings.

Once again we discover that God planned for creation to continue. Animals, like plants, were given God's blessing and the ability to reproduce more of their own kind.

God's creation is truly a continuing process. Children love animals. But do not assume that every child has had or will have an animal. Many children are not in a position to keep animals as pets. Boys and girls who live in the city may not come into contact with animals, except cats or dogs. Some children may be allergic to animals.

But even with these limitations, we can talk about being responsible for the other creatures that share God's creation. We can instill in boys and girls a sense of responsibility for animals. A child who has never held a baby animal does not know how gentle one must be to care for it. A child who has no respect for the creatures he or she shares the earth with, for instance, may not find it repulsive to torture a tortoise that finds itself stranded. This is the reason we must first help children to understand that they share God's world with these creatures and to see the importance of being kind to all creatures. Animals have needs of their own, in addition to contributing to our lives.

God created and filled the earth with many kinds of creatures.

Scope the ZONE

ZONE	TIME	SUPPLIES	⊚ ZILLIES®
Zoom Into the Zone			
Get in the Zone	5 minutes	page 174, cassette player	Cassette
Growing Animals	5 minutes	empty, clean, 10-ounce plastic soft drink bottles with lids; water	growing animals
BibleZone®			
Zoom Into the Bible	15 minutes	Bible for each student	none
Enjoy the Story	15 minutes	Reproducibles 8A, 8B, and 8C (top)	none
Bible Verse Blast	10 minutes	felt-tip marker, cassette player	balloons, Cassette
LifeZone			
Crazy Crab Relay	10 minutes	none	creature kickballs
Tiger Trouble	15 minutes	Reproducibles 8C (bottom) and 8D, scissors	none
Sing	5 minutes	Reproducible 8E, cassette player	Cassette
Sign 'n Praise	10 minutes	none	none

⊚ Zillies® are found in the **BibleZone® FUNspirational® Kit.**

Zoom Into the Zone

Choose one or more activities to catch your children's interest.

Supplies:
page 174,
cassette player

Zillies®:
Cassette

Get in the Zone

Have "The Bible Zone" **(Cassette)** playing as the students enter the room. Greet each student with a happy smile and **say: Welcome to the BibleZone!**

Give each student a copy of the words to "The Bible Zone" **(page 174).** Play the song again and invite everyone to sing with you.

Supplies:
empty, clean,
10-ounce plastic
soft drink bottles
with lids; water

Zillies®:
growing animals

Growing Animals

Ask: Have you ever taken care of an animal? What did you do? What do animals need to grow? *(Accept answers.)* **When God created the earth, God planned for many kinds of creatures. What decisions do you think God made about each creature as each one was created?** *(what it would look like, sound like, where it would live, what it would need to grow and live)*

Say: We can grow some unique animals of our own, and all we need is water in a bottle.

Give each student an empty, clean 10-ounce plastic soft drink container and one **growing animal.** Ask each student to name the animal he or she has.

Have the students drop the animals into the bottles and fill the bottles two-thirds full of water. Be sure they tighten the lids on the bottles.

Say: It will take a day or two to grow the animals, and it will be cool to see what happens. *(Note: The animals will expand and fill the bottles. Once the animal has expanded, the water can be poured out of the bottle.)*

> **God created and filled the earth with many kinds of creatures.**

Choose one or more activities to immerse your children in the Bible story.

Zoom Into the Bible

Be sure each student has a Bible. Ask everyone to read Genesis 1:20-25.

Supplies:
Bible for each student

Zillies®:
none

Say: **What did God command to come from the waters?** (*swarms of living creatures*)
What did God create birds to do? (*fly above the earth*)
What did God command the earth to bring forth? (*living creatures of every kind*)
How did God feel about creation? (*It was good.*)

Enjoy the Story

Tell or read the story "The Animals" **(Reproducibles 8A, 8B, and 8C, top). Ask:**
What do you think is important to animals? Why?
Do you think animals have feelings? Why?
Do you think animals have memory? Why?
Do you think there is a connection, an understanding, between people and animals? Why?
Are animals an important part of creation? Why?
Are animals important to you? Why?

Supplies:
Reproducibles 8A, 8B, and 8C (top)

Zillies®:
none

Bible Verse Blast

Write today's Bible verse on **balloons**, one word per balloon:
"LORD, you have made so many things! How wisely you made them all! The earth is filled with your creatures."

Supplies:
felt-tip marker, cassette player

Zillies®:
balloons, Cassette

Say: **Today's Bible verse is Psalm 104:24 from the** *Good News Bible.*

Ask everyone to say the verse with you.

Say: **I will toss the balloons in the air. Keep the balloons in the air while the music plays. When the music stops, grab a balloon. You will then have three minutes to get the words of the Bible verse in the correct order.**

The Animals

by Michael E. Williams

The stable was dark and cold. It smelled of hay and the animals who called it home. The quiet was disturbed by humans; a man and a woman, who have a donkey with them. The man is not old, but he is older than the woman. She looks like a young girl, and she looks very tired and sick. She laid down on the hay and groaned.

The donkey told the other animals the story. The couple had walked with him all the way from the north, near the Sea of Galilee. They had come to Bethlehem to get their names on the list to pay their taxes. This town was the man's family home, and he was the descendant of a great king.

"If he is part of the family of a great king, what is he doing staying in a stable?" the animals asked.

The donkey explained that the couple was neither royal nor wealthy anymore, even if their families had been long ago. The woman was going to have a baby and had ridden on the donkey's back most of the way. They had looked for other places to stay, but there were no rooms left anywhere in town. Finally, one kind person, seeing how tired and sick the young woman was, offered to let them stay in the stable.

"They must be riffraff," snorted the horse, who tended to be haughty and a bit high strung.

"I don't think so," the donkey answered. "They kept talking about how special the child the young woman was about to give birth to would be. An angel had told them that this child was the one God had intended to send from the beginning, the Messiah."

"From the beginning?" the animals gasped. They had heard stories of the beginning that had been passed down from their ancestors.

"How would a common donkey know the Messiah from a mushroom?" the horse sneered.

"Leave her alone." The cow defended the donkey. The cow tended to all the other animals and knew what it was like to be mother to others. "She's made a long journey. Besides, she was just telling us what she has heard."

"That's right," said the sheep who, being sheepish, usually didn't speak up. "Why do you act so high and mighty just because you're a horse?"

"You tell him," crowed the rooster, keeping the sheep between himself and the horse's hooves. "We all know that there's only one way to know if this is the One sent from God. Someone will just have to ask him if he remembers that day."

The animals' conversation was interrupted by the piercing cry of a baby. When they looked around the wall of the stall, they saw the young woman cradling a tiny bundle in her arms.

She still looked tired, but now there was a look of sheer joy on her face that shone through the weariness. The man was smiling too. He spent

Reproducible 8A

BIBLEZONE®

his time making the young woman and the baby as comfortable as possible.

When the man looked for a place to lay the baby so they could all get some sleep, he found none. Finally he put fresh straw into the manger where the animals would have normally been fed. After the baby had nursed and finally went to sleep, the man placed him ever so gently into the manger. Then the man went back and held his wife to keep the chill of the stable from making her sick. After a time they both were warm enough that they fell asleep.

That's when the animals began to move toward the manger to get a better look at the little intruder into their stable. The cow and the donkey stood on either side of the feed trough, while the rooster perched on the very edge above the baby's head. The horse kept his distance and looked straight down his nose at the tiny child. What they could see of his skin was red and wrinkled. They could see very little, though, since he was wrapped in bands of cloth called swaddling cloths. None of them had ever seen a baby that close before.

"Shall we wake him to ask our question or wait until he awakens on his own?" asked the sheep.

"I think we should wait," the cow spoke up. "Getting born is no easy thing to do, you know."

So they waited and watched. Finally the baby began to stir. Before he could make enough noise to awaken the sleeping woman and man, the cow spoke.

"Hello there, little one," she began.

"Hello there, big one," the child replied. As is usual with newborn babies and animals, the child spoke to the cow with his eyes

and his mind, not his mouth.

"Do you remember me?" the cow continued.

"Remember you?" the infant repeated.

"Think hard. It was a long time ago, when things were just getting started. Our ancestors passed the oral tradition along to us. God was telling a long beautiful story called Creation. In the middle we appeared, the animals, that is. At first we thought that God had been all alone before we appeared. That made us feel very important, indeed."

"Get on with it," the horse interrupted impatiently. "The child isn't going to remember us anyway."

"Don't be so sure, and don't be so hasty," the cow replied in a calm but determined voice. Then turning back to the manger she continued. "Then when we thought about the situation, it just didn't make sense that God would be telling a story to no one. So the animals decided that God must be telling this story for a child. Were you that child? Were you with God at the creation of the world?"

The infant looked the cow directly in the eye, and his mind formed only a single phrase. "It is good," was that phrase.

The minute they heard it, all the animals knelt down by the manger, even the horse. This was the child the world, and they, had been waiting for. Only one who had been with God at the very beginning of the world would have known the phrase God had used to describe every single stage of the story. This baby with only a manger for a bed and a stable for a nursery was the chosen one of God.

Reproducible 8B

So the animals added another story to their oral history. It is known in their tradition simply as "The Stable Story," but all the animals know. It is a special favorite of the younger ones. They tell how the animals were the first to recognize that Jesus was the chosen one of God, the one who had been present at the creation.

Human legends say that the animals tell this particular story at just about midnight on Christmas Eve night. When they get to the point that the animals in the story kneel to honor the Christ Child, the animals in the stable do the same. If you happen to be out in the stable at midnight on Christmas Eve night, you can see them.

At least, that's what they say.

Reproducible 8C

BibleZone®

Choose one or more activities to bring the Bible to life.

Crazy Crab Relay

Supplies:
none

Zillies®:
creature kickballs

(D)ivide the students into three teams and have the teams line up on one side of the classroom.

Say: **God made many kinds of creatures. We are going to have a relay to find out which team has the fastest creature.**

Have one student from each team get on the floor in a crab walk position (sit on floor with hands and feet on floor, lift body off of floor). Place a **creature kickball** on the floor in front of each player's feet.

Say: **When I yell "Go!" kick your creature kickball toward the wall on the opposite side of the room, crab walk to the ball, kick it again, and continue crab walking and kicking until your creature kickball hits the wall on the opposite side of the room. When it does, you must turn around and crab walk and kick the ball back to your team. The next player on your team then has to crab walk and kick the ball to the wall and back again. The team who has all its players finish the relay first wins. You must crab walk all the time, and you cannot touch the creature kickballs with anything but your feet.**

Tiger Trouble

Supplies:
Reproducibles 8C (bottom) and 8D, scissors

Zillies®:
none

(M)ake four photocopies of the animal cards **(Reproducibles 8C, bottom, and 8D)** to make a set of playing cards. Four to six students may play with a set of cards at time. (You may need to make extra sets if you have several students.)

Remove one of the tiger cards and shuffle the remaining cards. Deal the cards one at a time around the table to each player until the whole set is dealt out. Have the players sort their cards into pairs and place their pairs on the table in front of them, face up. (Four cards of a kind become two pairs.)

The first player offers his or her remaining cards face down, and spread out like a fan, to the player on the left, who draws one. If the card drawn makes a pair, the pair is placed face up in front of the second player. That player, whether a pair was made or not, then offers the cards remaining in his or her hands face down to the player on the left. This is continued until only one card is left, which will be the odd tiger card.

Choose one or more activities to bring the Bible to life.

Supplies:
Reproducible 8E,
cassette player

Zillies®:
Cassette

Supplies:
none

Zillies®:
none

Sing

Give each student a copy of the words to the song "Make a Big Splash" **(Reproducible 8E).** Play the song on the **Cassette** and ask everyone to listen. **Ask: Do you suppose God created animals to make a big splash?**

Sign 'n Praise

Say: When God created all the creatures of the earth, God saw that it was good.

Teach everyone how to sign the phrase, "And God saw that it was good."

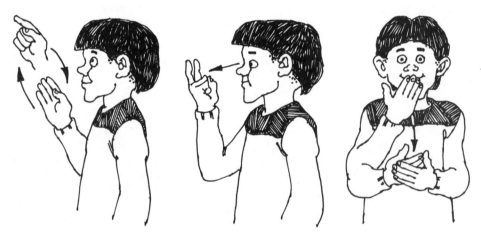

Lead the students in the following litany:
God said, "Let the waters bring forth swarms of living creatures, and let birds fly above the earth across the dome of the sky."
So God created the great sea monsters and every living creature that moves of every kind, with which the waters swarm, and every winged bird of every kind.
(Sign "And God saw that it was good.")
God said, "Let the earth bring forth living creatures of every kind: cattle and creeping things and wild animals of the earth of every kind."
God made the wild animals of the earth of every kind, and everything that creeps upon the ground of every kind.
(Sign "And God saw that it was good.")

Give each student a copy of HomeZone® to enjoy this week.

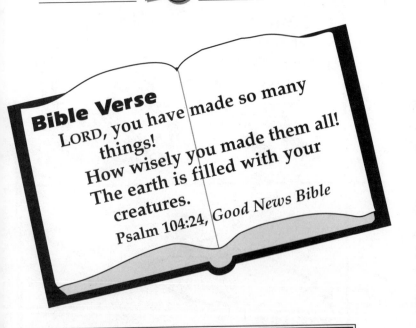

Bible Verse

LORD, you have made so many things!
How wisely you made them all!
The earth is filled with your creatures.

Psalm 104:24, Good News Bible

Did You Know?

God created each animal with unique characteristics. Each one is just right for the place it lives and the foods it eats.

Did you know a flying squirrel cannot really fly? It uses the skin that stretches between its legs like a parachute to glide from tree to tree.

Did you know that a fly's taste organs are in its feet? If a fly lands on sugar, it will stamp its feet to be sure the sugar can be eaten. Then the fly will begin its meal.

Did you know that the arctic fox has tiny ears that lose little heat in the icy north? The desert fox has large ears so that it can lose heat and keep cool in the desert!

Turtle Cake

You will need:
German chocolate cake mix
one (14-ounce) package caramels
¾ cup margarine
1 cup chopped pecans
one 6-ounce package semi-sweet chocolate chips
½ cup evaporated milk

Preheat oven to 350 degrees. Prepare the cake mix according to package directions. Grease and flour a 9-by-13-inch pan. Pour half of the cake mix into the pan and bake for 15 minutes.

While baking, melt the caramels in a pan with the margarine and milk. Pour the hot caramel mixture over the cake. Sprinkle the chocolate chips and pecans over the caramel. Pour the remaining cake batter over the chocolate chips and pecans and bake for another 20 minutes.

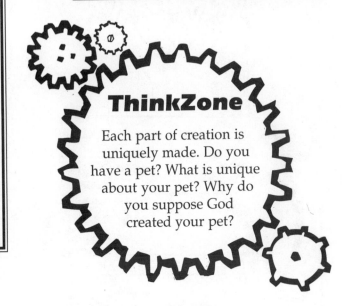

ThinkZone

Each part of creation is uniquely made. Do you have a pet? What is unique about your pet? Why do you suppose God created your pet?

God created and filled the earth with many kinds of creatures.

103

Reproducible 8D

BIBLEZONE®

Make a Big Splash

Make a big splash in God's world
Make a big splash
Make a big splash in God's world
Make a big splash

Every otter gotta splash in the water
Every otter oughtta slide down the riverside
God makes the rain, the rain makes the river
The river makes every otter wanna make a big splash
Make a big splash in God's world
Make a big splash

Gotta love God's world, every otter oughtta
Soak up the sunshine, slip in the water
Gotta love God's world, every otter knows it
The bigger the splash, the more an otter shows it

Every animal does what it oughtta
Swimmin', divin', splashin' in the water
God makes the rain, the rain makes the river
The river makes animals wanna make a big splash
Make a big splash in God's world
Make a big splash

Gotta love God's world, gotta love the water
Find a new friend and play like an otter
Gotta love God's world, gotta love the giver
Everybody shows it down by the river

Everybody does what they oughtta
Swimmin', divin', splashin' in the water
God makes the rain, the rain makes the river
The river makes animals wanna make a big splash
Make a big splash in God's world
Make a big splash in God's world
In God's world, in God's world
Make a big splash in God's world.
Make a big splash in God's world.

Words and music by Tom Steinman and Jay Tyler
Copyright © 1997 Bridge Building Music/BMI and New Spring Publishing/ASCAP.
All rights reserved.
Used by permssion of Brentwood-Benson Music Publishing, Inc.
From the Brentwood-Benson Music Publishing, Inc. recording *God's Wacky Animals*.

Reproducible 8E

105

In God's Image

Enter the **ZONE**®

Bible Verse
So God created humankind in his image.
Genesis 1:27

Bible Story
Genesis 1:26-31

The Creation Hymn in Genesis is so much more than a step-by-step record of the appearance of life on earth. This Scripture is a celebration of human beings as the magnificent completion of God's plan of creation. Of all that God created, only human beings—made in the image of God—did God pronounce "very good."

Humans are different from any of the other living creatures. They share the spiritual characteristics of God that no other creature shares. Humans can think, remember, make plans for the future, choose, create, and reflect on their experiences. Human beings rise above their animal instincts for survival to care about the survival of others.

Humans are spiritual beings. They can worship God and experience feelings of awe and wonder. They can appreciate God's world and live in fellowship with God, who is Spirit, and with other human beings. Like no other creatures, humans can pray to God and can receive and understand God's answers within their spiritual selves.

When we talk about the image of God, first we have to get beyond the idea of physical characteristics. Obviously, as the boys and girls look around themselves, they see people who are a variety of sizes, shapes, and colors. So which group, they will ask, represents the image of God? We will answer, "They all do!" God has given people the ability to choose, not merely to act on instinct or training. The choices humans make determine how they reflect God's image.

Older elementary boys and girls often seek affirmation of themselves as persons. They will identify with the group that gives them this affirmation. Make it a point to emphasize the specialness of each child in your group. Help your students understand that our similarities relate us to one another, and our differences relate us to God.

They can also understand that we are also related through our Christian faith. They can understand and identify themselves as Christians. Through our faith as adults and through our beliefs and actions as Christians, we can help boys and girls know that all people are children of God. God is our Creator.

106

God created humankind in God's image.

Scope the ZONE

ZONE	TIME	SUPPLIES	⊚ ZILLIES
Zoom Into the Zone			
Get in the Zone	5 minutes	page 174, cassette player	Cassette
Brainteaser Bingo	10 minutes	Reproducible 9C, pens or pencils	none
BibleZone®			
Zoom Into the Bible	15 minutes	Bible for each student	none
Enjoy the Story	15 minutes	Reproducibles 9A and 9B	none
Bible Verse Volley	5 minutes	Bible	none
LifeZone			
Fabulous Features	15 minutes	Reproducible 9D, multi-cultural crayons or pencils	none
Life-Size Gallery	15 minutes	butcher paper, tape, pencils, scissors, markers	none
Sing	5 minutes	Reproducible 9E, cassette player	Cassette
Praise	10 minutes	none	yarn

⊚ Zillies® are found in the **BibleZone® FUNspirational® Kit.**

Zoom Into the Zone

Choose one or more activities to catch your children's interest.

Supplies:
page 174,
cassette player

Zillies®:
Cassette

Get in the Zone

Greet each student enthusiastically. **Say: Welcome to the BibleZone! Here we have fun while we are learning about God and about what God wants for our lives.**

Play "The Bible Zone" **(Cassette)** and invite everyone to sing with you. Have copies of the words **(page 174)** available for anyone who needs them.

Supplies:
Reproducible 9C,
pens or pencils

Zillies®:
none

Brainteaser Bingo

Give each student a photocopy of the bingo card **(Reproducible 9C)** and a pen or pencil. Ask the students to scatter out so that they cannot see one another's cards.

Say: In each square write a description of someone in the group without naming that person. For example, you might write "wears braces" or "has red hair" or "plays the tuba."

After the students have had time to fill in the squares, collect the papers. Shuffle them. Pass the papers out again.

Ask the students to go around the room and request the autographs of the boys or girls who match the descriptions written on the squares.

Say: Just as in the game of bingo, the first person to fill a vertical column is a winner. So are the first persons to fill a horizontal column, a diagonal line, all four corners, and the entire sheet of paper.

When the game is over, **ask: What are some of the things we discovered about each other? How are we alike? How are we different?**

Say: Today we are going to learn from the Bible that God created us in God's image. Let's find out what that means.

 God created humankind in God's image.

Choose one or more activities to immerse your children in the Bible story.

Zoom Into the Bible

e sure each student has a Bible. Ask everyone to read Genesis 1:26-31.

Say: **What did God create?** *(humankind)*
How did God create humankind? *(in God's image)*
What did God create as humankind? *(male and female)*
How did God feel about creation? *(It was very good.)*

Say: **This Scripture is a celebration of human beings as the magnificent completion of God's plan of creation. Of all that God created, only human beings—made in the image of God—did God pronounce "very good.**

Supplies:
Bible for each student

Zillies®:
none

Enjoy the Story

ell or read the story "In God's Image" **(Reproducibles 9A and 9B).** Ask:
When we say we are made in God's image, do we mean physical resemblance?
Could we possibly think of something that God has not already thought of? Why?

Say: **How awesome to know that each of us is created in God's image! Every human being is a child of God, created in God's image. We have been created with the ability to love, to empathize, to care, to feel compassion, and to choose between good and evil. All human beings have this gift. We were created to reflect God as we relate to one another.**

Supplies:
Reproducibles 9A and 9B

Zillies®:
none

Bible Verse Volley

sk a student to read Genesis 1:27 in the Bible: "So God created humankind in his image."

Divide the class into two teams. Have the teams stand facing one another. Ask them to take turns, one team saying the Bible verse and the opposite team saying the verse backwards. Switch back and forth until both teams can say the verse both ways.

Supplies:
Bible

Zillies®:

In God's Image

by Michael E. Williams

A long time ago teachers, called rabbis or sages, told stories to help people understand different passages of Scripture. These stories were called midrashim (or a midrash, if there is only one such story). They were often included in sermons or lessons and then later were written down so we can still read some of them today. This story is based upon a midrash on the creation.

When God began to create all that there is, many things came to be. It was as if God was telling a story that became the universe. As soon as the words rolled off God's tongue, they became the very things they described. When God said "light," there was light. When God said "land," there was land. When God said "sun, moon, and stars," these lights began to do their dance around the heavens. When God said "plants and animals," you know what happened. Everything God spoke came to be.

When the story was nearly done, God felt that there was still something missing. Of all the characters of creation there was none creative enough to say that they were like God. In other words there was not a creature who could tell a story back to God.

So God said, "Let us create a character who is like us. Let us create a character in the divine image."

Us! That's right. The original story has God speaking in the plural. Who is us? The Bible doesn't say, but the ancient rabbis used their imaginations and guessed who God might have been talking to. Some say it was the other creatures, that God was enlisting the help of the rest of creation in making this new creature.

Others, though, said that God was talking to the heavenly host, the angels. And these same rabbis suggest that the angels didn't like what they heard. They saw a danger in making a character who was too much like God, for that creature would have entirely too much freedom.

"Oh, you don't want to do a thing like that," the angel of the night objected. "If you create beings too much like you, they will use my darkness to cover the terrible deeds they might do. They could break into houses and rob people or do even worse under the cover of darkness."

"True," God replied, "but to be like me they would have to be free to make the wrong choices. Otherwise they could not freely make the right choices."

Then the angel of the air piped up, "If you make beings like you, they will learn to build fires and fill my air with smoke so that no one will be able to even see the sky."

"Without the secret of fire," God asked the angel, "how will they cook their food and keep warm in the winter?"

Then the angel of the waters chimed in, "If you do this thing you are planning to do, these creatures will be able to dirty my rivers and lakes and oceans with their trash until the water will not be fit for anything."

Reproducible 9A

BibleZone®

"That may just be a chance we have to take," God replied. The angels could see that the creator of the universe was determined.

So one of the angels took another approach to the subject. "If you create beings with so much freedom, then they will be free to create schools and universities and research institutes. They will invent microscopes and telescopes and will explore all the secrets of your creation. Before long they will discover molecules and atoms and subatomic particles. They will find stars invisible to the ordinary eye. Even black holes and quarks will be no mystery to them. They will be able to ferret out every secret you have woven into every fabric of the universe."

"So?" was God's only reply. The divine patience was running out with all this discussion of what might happen.

Even so another angel added to the warning. "You realize, don't you, that these creatures would soon discover medicines. Then would come those who studied these medicines. Some would know what medicine to give for any ailment. Others would learn to open the body and repair its parts. Before long they would replace those parts with other body parts and even machines that they have invented. These creatures would live longer and longer until there is no telling how long they will live."

"Long life is not a bad thing, if it is lived well," was God's only reply. There was an edge of irritation in the divine voice.

One more angel made one more attempt. "Creatures with so much freedom to be creative will soon learn to imitate you. They will be painting portraits of the other creatures and themselves. They will hear the sounds of your universe and put them together in different patterns, then call it music. They will move in imitation of the swaying of trees in the wind or the easy rolling walk of a cat on a stroll and call it dance. They will learn to tell and write stories and call it literature. They will act out those stories and call it theatre. The stories about your universe they will call philosophy. Then the stories they tell about you they will call theology."

"Don't you understand?" God interrupted. "That's the idea. They are supposed to be creative like I am creative. They are supposed to be playful like I'm playful. They are supposed to enjoy this wonder-filled story I have told as much as I do."

"But," added the angel in a last-ditch effort to talk God out of this plan. "What if they think of something you haven't thought of?"

At that God leaned back and let out a hearty laugh, pounding large divine hands against the chest from which emerged the heartbeat of the universe and said with obvious delight, "Well, then, I'll just have to say that my children have done better than even I could do."

Then the rabbis say that God created human beings in the divine image. Both males and females were created with the freedom to choose to become what God had dreamed of them becoming all along.

Reproducible 9B

Reproducible 9C

BibleZone®

Fabulous Features

Supplies:
Reproducible 9D, multicultural crayons or pencils

Zillies®:
none

Give each student a photocopy of the picture of the boys and girls playing a game **(Reproducible 9D)**. Read today's Bible verse that is on the picture. Invite the students to color the picture and to consider the hair color, eye color, and skin color of each boy or girl. Ask them to write beside each figure the name of a person of whom the picture reminds them.

Ask: What are the fabulous features of each of these people? How is each of these people created in God's image? (*Give each student time to respond thoughtfully.*) **Why do you suppose they all look so happy?**

Life-Size Gallery

Supplies:
butcher paper, tape, pencils, markers, scissors

Zillies®:
none

Ask: **What is an image?** (*a likeness of something that closely resembles the original*) **Where might you see an image?** (*in something that reflects, like a mirror*) **What do mirrors tell us?** (*what we look like*) **If we are created in the image of God, does that mean we all look like God?** (*No, we are created to resemble God in our actions and our choices.*)

Say: Let's create a life-size gallery and think about ways we are created in the image of God.

Find ways to pair the students; for example, matching hair color, matching eye color, matching height, matching colors of clothing, matching shoes, and so forth.

Have butcher paper that you can cut to fit the height of each student. Lay the paper on the floor.

Say: Pairs should work together to create a life-size gallery. One person should lie on the paper while the other person traces around him or her. You can lie in whatever position you please. After you have traced around your bodies, write your name on your drawing.

Tape the outlines on the walls around the room. **Say: Look at each drawing. Write one physical characteristic on each drawing. Then think about how that person reflects the image of God in his or her actions and choices. Write one way on each outline.**

Supplies:
Reproducible 9E,
cassette player

Zillies®:
Cassette

Sing

Give each student a copy of the words to the song "He's Got the Whole World in His Hands" **(Reproducible 9E).** Play the song on the **Cassette** and ask everyone to follow along. Play the song again and invite everyone to sing with you.

Ask: Why do you think God has the whole world in God's hands?

Supplies:
none

Zillies®:
yarn

Praise

Say: Human beings were the last thing that God created. Human beings were the only thing that God pronounced as "very good." God made human beings who could think out things, design and make new things, anticipate problems and work out solutions, share ideas with one another, and enjoy all that God had created. God created human beings to be like God—not in the way we look—but in the ways we think and feel and act.

Have **yarn** wrapped in a ball. Ask everyone to stand in a circle.

Say: God created human beings in the image of God. Sometimes the things we do are not good reflections of what God is like. So today let's ask God to help us live in God's image. I will toss the ball of yarn to one of you. You will say, "God help me to be . . ." and then name something that will help you reflect God in your actions and choices. For example, I might say, "Help me to be more patient." After you say your part of the prayer, hold onto the yarn and toss the ball of yarn to another person. Let's continue until everyone has added to our prayer.

End by praying: Thank you, God, for helping us to reflect your image in all that we do. Amen.

 God created humankind in God's image.

Give each student a copy of HomeZone® to enjoy this week.

Home 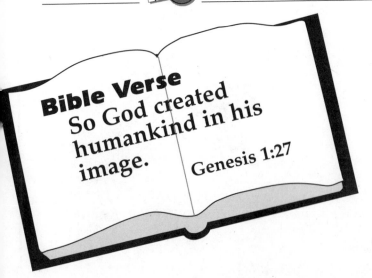 For Students

Bible Verse
So God created humankind in his image.
Genesis 1:27

Clay Necklaces

Use the following recipe to make clay. Use small lumps of clay to make small balls. Push a toothpick through the center of each ball. When the clay has dried thoroughly, use acrylic paint to paint the balls. When the paint has dried thoroughly, use a leather or gold cord to make a necklace. Plan to give your necklace to someone special.

Clay Recipe
1 cup cornstarch
1¼ cups water
2 cups baking soda (1-lb. box)
Cook the mixture until it thickens to a dough-like consistency. Turn the mixture out on a pastry board and knead. Cover with a damp cloth or store in a plastic bag.

Gingerbread Cutout Cookies

You will need:
½ cup shortening
⅓ cup sugar
½ cup molasses
¼ cup water
2½ cups all-purpose flour
½ tsp. soda
¾ tsp. ginger
¼ tsp. nutmeg
¼ tsp. cinnamon

Cream shortening and sugar. Blend flour, soda, ginger, nutmeg, and cinnamon and add to shortening mixture. Add water and molasses. Mix well. Cover and chill 2 to 3 hours. Heat oven to 350 degrees. Roll dough on a lightly floured board or surface until it is about ¼-inch thick. If dough is sticky, add a little flour. Cut out cookies using people-shaped cookie cutters. Place the cookies on an ungreased cookie sheet. Bake for 10 minutes. Remove from the cookie sheet immediately. Makes about 15 4-inch cookies.

ThinkZone
Sometime when you are at the mall or the grocery store, be a people watcher. Notice how each person is unique—culture, race, age? What image of God do you see in each person?

 **God created humankind in God's image.**

 115

So God created humankind in his image.

Genesis 1:27

Reproducible 9D

BibleZone®

He's Got the Whole World in His Hands

He's got the whole world in His hands
He's got the whole world in His hands
He's got the whole world in His hands
He's got the whole world in His hands

He's got the wind and the rain in His hands
He's got the wind and the rain in His hands
He's got the wind and the rain in His hands
He's got the whole world in His hands

He's got the tiny little baby in His hands
He's got the tiny little baby in His hands
He's got the tiny little baby in His hands
He's got the whole world in His hands

He's got you and me, brother, in His hands
He's got you and me, sister, in His hands
He's got you and me, brother, in His hands
He's got the whole world in His hands

He's got the whole world in His hands
He's got the whole world in His hands
He's got the whole world in His hands
He's got the whole world in his hands

Reproducible 9E

Adam and Eve

Enter the

Bible Verse
God made us, and we belong to God.

Psalm 100:3, *Good News Bible*, adapted

Bible Story
Genesis 2:4-9, 15-18, 21-23, 25; 3:1-13

A careful reader will discover that there are actually two creation stories in the Book of Genesis. The first story (Genesis 1:1–2:4) culminates with the creation of human beings as one act (Genesis 1:27) and the directive to have dominion over all that God created. In the second creation story (Genesis 2:5–4:26), the creation of humankind is in two stages, but is not complete until man and woman are standing in partnership with each other.

The story that includes Adam and Eve and the Garden of Eden is a colorful story, filled with rich, memorable images—Adam's formation from the dust of the earth, Eve's creation from one of Adam's ribs, a magnificent garden of delights, a Tree of Life, a wily serpent, and an angel with a fiery sword. Through these stories the Hebrew people tried to answer some of their most basic questions: Why do human beings, created in the image of God, refuse to acknowledge the sovereignty of their Creator? How did evil come into such a perfect creation?

The stories concerning ancient history cannot be regarded as exact factual accounts of the sort that today's modern historian or

scientist might produce. They *are* historical in that they communicate, however, the *meaning* of history. The writer of these stories emphasized that God was the Supreme Ruler of the universe and that all living creatures were dependent upon God. The writer also explained that throughout the life of all humankind, even at the very beginning of things, human beings have always been a rebellious and prideful lot, quick to turn away from God.

In the second part of the Creation story, we see a God who is concerned with humanity. This story focuses not on a God who creates with mighty commands, but on one who nurtures from the dust the creature, man, with whom God chooses to be in relationship. This story emphasizes God's loving and caring nature. Older elementary boys and girls need to know that they are not the results of random acts of science. Of all the living things that God created, only human beings can plan, choose, remember, pray, worship, imagine, and create. Human beings are definitely very special parts of God's creation.

God made all people.

Scope the ZONE

ZONE	TIME	SUPPLIES	⊚ ZILLIES
Zoom Into the Zone			
Get in the Zone	5 minutes	page 174, cassette player	Cassette
Perfect Partners	10 minutes	none	none
BibleZone®			
All-Alone Adam	10 minutes	none	atom ball
Zoom Into the Bible	20 minutes	Bible for each student	none
Enjoy the Story	15 minutes	Reproducibles 10A and 10B	none
LifeZone			
Bible Verse Scramble	10 minutes	Reproducible 10C, scissors	none
Positive Identification	10 minutes	Reproducible 10D, pens or markers, ink pads with washable ink	none
Sing	5 minutes	Reproducible 10E, cassette player	Cassette
Sign 'n Praise	10 minutes	none	none

⊚ Zillies® are found in the **BibleZone® FUNspirational® Kit.**

Zoom Into the Zone

Choose one or more activities to catch your children's interest.

Supplies:
page 174,
cassette player

Zillies®:
Cassette

Get in the Zone

Greet each student enthusiastically. **Say: Welcome to the BibleZone! Here we have fun while we are learning about God and about what God wants for our lives.**

Play "The Bible Zone" **(Cassette)** and invite everyone to sing with you. Have copies of the words **(page 174)** available for anyone who needs them.

Supplies:
none

Zillies®:
none

Perfect Partners

Ask everyone to sit on the floor in a large circle. **Say: Put your feet on the floor in front of you with your knees up. When I say "Go!", try to stand up without putting your hands on the floor.**

If any students have been able to stand up, ask them to sit down in their original position without using their hands.

Say: Now let's see what happens when we have a partner to help us. Ask the students to turn to a person beside them to create partners.

Say: Sit on the floor and face your partner. Keep your feet flat on the floor and your toes touching. Reach forward and grab hands. Now, help each other stand up.

Then ask everyone to sit down using the same movements.

Next have the partners sit back to back on the floor. Ask the students to bring their knees up close to their chests.

Say: Push your backs against each other and try to stand up. Do not use any hands.

When any partners stand up, have them sit down using the same movements.

Say: Everyone knows that working together makes a job easier. The Bible tells us that God created the first human beings. God gave them a beautiful garden named Eden where they could live. They had everything they needed. They were perfect partners. God cared for them, and they belonged to God.

120

Choose one or more activities to immerse your children in the Bible story.

All-Alone Adam

Supplies:
none

Zillies®:
atom ball

Have everyone stand in a circle. Select one student to be Adam, the first human being. **Say: When God created the first human being, he was all alone. Let's see if Adam can find a partner for him.**

Have Adam walk around the outside of the circle. Have the students stand with their hands open behind their backs. Have Adam say, "I am alone. I need a partner. I wonder who it will be."

As Adam goes around the circle, have him or her drop an **atom ball** in someone's hand. That person must chase Adam around the circle. If Adam can get back to that person's space before Adam has been tagged, that person becomes Adam.

Zoom Into the Bible

Supplies:
Bible for each student

Zillies®:
none

Be sure each student has a Bible. Divide the following verses to be read: Genesis 2:4-9, 15-18, 21-23, 25; 3:1-13. **Ask:**
What did God create from the dust of the ground? (*man*)
What special tree did God put in the Garden of Eden? (*the tree of the knowledge of good and evil*)
What did God forbid the man to do? (*eat from the tree of good and evil*)
What did God decide to do for man? (*make a partner for him*)
How did God create the partner? (*from the man's rib*)
What did the man call his partner? (*woman*)
What did the serpent convince the woman to do? (*eat from the tree in the middle of the garden—the tree of the knowledge of good and evil*)
What happened when the man and the woman ate from the tree? (*They knew they were naked and made clothes from fig leaves.*)
What excuse did the man give to God? (*The woman gave him the fruit.*)
What excuse did the woman give to God? (*The serpent tricked her.*)

Enjoy the Story

Supplies:
Reproducibles 10A and 10B

Zillies®:
none

Tell or read the story "Adam and Eve" **(Reproducibles 10A and 10B).** **Ask: Why do you suppose Adam and Eve ate from the tree? How did things change between Adam and Eve? between Adam and Eve and God?**

Adam and Eve

by Michael E. Williams

He says: I was just feeling a little lonely, that's all. I wanted some company. So I took my request to you, God, since you were the only other person I really knew at the time. Besides, you were behind the whole operation, as far as I could see.

Speaking of operation! The next thing I knew, I was waking up in the recovery room with an ache in my side where I used to think my heart used to be. And there beside me was the most wondrous creature I had ever seen.

She (I wasn't sure then why I called her that) was not like any of the other creatures. She was just like me, only a little different. And the differences were what made all the difference. I thought she was just great. I broke into song.

Bone of my bone
And flesh of my flesh,
You are called woman,
And I am called man.

It wasn't a really great song, I have to admit. It didn't even rhyme. But I wasn't too experienced at talking to other people at the time. Other than you, that is.

She says: I didn't know where I was at first. I awoke to the worst singing I had ever heard. Well, it was the *first* singing I had ever heard, but it was pretty bad. I thought the other creature was in pain. I saw the wound in his side and thought he had to be injured.

He was full of pretty words at first, though. He told me he had been injured so he could be with me. He told me that God had taken out

his heart and given it to me. Later I found out it was a rib. He was a sweet talker from the first. What he never seemed to grasp was that I had no say so in the deal at all. I didn't ask to be born. I didn't ask to be paired up with him. It was the way he wanted it from the first. And believe me, he liked things his way.

He says: From the start she loved to walk around the garden, and I admit it is beautiful. There seemed to be no harm in it. You had told us both which tree to avoid. The one in the middle of the garden named the Tree of the Knowledge of Good and Evil. It seemed like a pretty impressive name for a fairly ordinary-looking tree. All the same, you said don't eat its fruit, so we stayed away from it.

Until that morning we were out for a walk, and she ran into the serpent. Oh, he was a smooth talker. He seemed so smart and well-informed about everything. He was able to use the scientific names for the plants and knew the history of the garden about as well as you. No offense, I know he didn't make it, but he did seem to know a lot about it.

When the serpent offered her the fruit, and it looked so good, she ate it. She didn't want to at first. In fact she argued with him about it, but the fruit looked so good, and the snake really seemed to know what he was talking about.

It tasted good too. I mean, she tasted it first, then handed it to me. I didn't know what to do. Since she didn't die right away, it seemed all right for me to eat some. And I didn't die right away. The woman you created made me do it.

Reproducible 10A

BibleZone®

She says: It was just a day like any other day. We had gone for a walk through the garden. The serpent was out and about. We had seen him there many times. We both enjoyed talking to him. He was so smart. He knew something about everything.

That day he wanted to talk about the tree. You know, the tree. The one you told us not to eat from. The serpent started with a question. "Why? Why were we put here in this garden and told not to eat from any of the trees?" That's what he asked.

Well, for the first time I felt that I knew something the serpent didn't, because that is not what you had said. So I told him that you hadn't told us not to eat from any of the trees. You had told us not to eat from that one tree in the middle of the garden. I added that we shouldn't even touch it, even though you hadn't really said that. I figured that if we didn't touch it, it certainly couldn't hurt us.

What would happen if we did eat, he asked. Oh, we would die, I answered. He laughed and said, "You won't die. You'll become just like God, able to know good from evil. You'll be able to make choices about everything in your life. Taste it, it's good."

I really didn't know what choices were at the time, but it sounded like it might be fun to make them. So I tasted the fruit, and it was good. It was to die for, as they say. I honestly waited to die right then and there. But I didn't. I never thought that you might have meant that we would die eventually. I always thought we would drop dead on the spot, the minute we tasted it. I never imagined that it would plant the seed of death within us, which would only come to flower in our old age.

The man ate, as well. The only thing that changed at that moment was the way he looked at me. When he looked at me, my cheeks turned hot, and I wanted to cover my body. I had never had these feelings before. We had never worn clothes. We had never felt a need to. I was ashamed and went and tried to make clothes from the leaves of one of the trees of the garden. It was the first of my choices, and it didn't work very well.

You see, the serpent you put in the garden tricked me into eating it.

He says: Have you ever wished you hadn't done something, but knew it was too late to wish it away? That's how I feel. Why am I trying to tell you how I feel? You know.

Now I feel a distance between us, you and I, that I never felt before. And there is a distance between the woman and me, as well. I have to watch what I say to her, or I hurt her feelings or make her feel ashamed. She is guarded about what she says to me too, I can tell.

For the first time I feel really lonely, and that is even worse than the shame.

She says: Once there was a garden and you and the man and me. We were all together, all one. Now we are separate parts of some great design that only you seem to know.

I speak to the man, and he walks away offended. Or I try to comfort him, and he will not be comforted. Often there is silence between us. Before the silence was something we shared, that wrapped us together like a blanket. Now it keeps us apart like a wall.

Where do we go from here? I guess that is another of those choices. More important than that: will you go with us as we leave this place?

Reproducible 10B

God	made
us,	and
we	belong
to	God.
God	made
us,	and
we	belong
to	God.

Reproducible 10C

BibleZone®

Bible Verse Scramble

Supplies:
Reproducible 10C,
scissors

Zillies®:
none

Divide the class into teams of three or four students. Make enough photocopies of the Bible verse cards **(Reproducible 10C)** that there is a set for each team.

Say: Our Bible verse for today is the third verse of Psalm 100, adapted from the *Good News Bible:* "God made us, and we belong to God."

Invite everyone to say the verse with you. Scramble all the sets of Bible verse cards and spread them out on a table. Challenge the teams to find the words of the Bible verse and put them in the correct order. To increase the challenge repeat and have the teams try to improve their time. Also turn the cards face down.

Positive Identification

Supplies:
Reproducible 10D,
pens or markers,
ink pads with
washable ink

Zillies®:
none

Give each student a photocopy of the certificate **(Reproducible 10D)**. **Ask: Do you know one way that a positive identification can be made of each person?** *(fingerprints)*

Say: When God created each of us, God made each of us unique. God gave each of us fingerprints that are like no others. When we look at our fingerprints, we not only know we are unique, but we know that God made us, and we belong to God.

Invite the students to write on their certificates and to add their fingerprints.

Sing

Supplies:
Reproducible 10E,
cassette player

Zillies®:
Cassette

Give each student a copy of the words to the song "He's Got the Whole World in His Hands" **(Reproducible 10E)**. Play the song on the **Cassette** and ask everyone to listen. Play the song again and invite everyone to sing with you.

Supplies:
none

Zillies®:
none

Sign 'n Praise

each the students the American Sign Language for today's Bible verse.

Say: On the sixth day of creation God created human beings. God created the man named Adam. Then God created the woman named Eve. God placed them in a beautiful garden where they had everything they could possibly want. God cared for them and loved them, and they belonged to God.

Once the students become familiar with the signs, have them stand in a circle and sign around the circle. Have the first student sign the word *God.* Have the second student sign the word *made;* the third the word *us,* and so forth until the verse has been completely signed around the circle. (You also could play a game of popcorn by allowing each student as he or she signs a word to say the name of the next person who will sign.)

Close with a friendship circle. Bring all the students shoulder to shoulder. Have them put their arms over the shoulders of the persons next to them, forming a huddle. Lean forward.

Pray: Dear God, you made us and we belong to you. (*Count "One, two, three," and break the circle.*)

Give each student a copy of HomeZone® to enjoy this week.

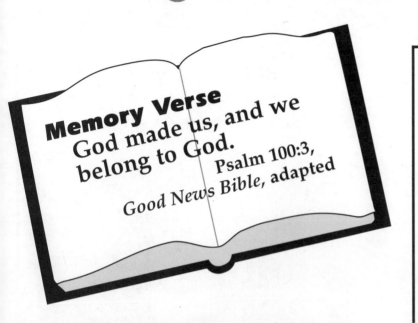

Memory Verse
God made us, and we belong to God.
Psalm 100:3,
Good News Bible, adapted

Fingerprint Cards

You can I.D. everyone in your family by making thumbprint cards. Use a 4-by-6 index card for each person. Write the person's name and the date on each card.

Draw ten boxes on the card. Label them: right thumb, right index, right middle, right ring, right little; left thumb, left index, left middle, left ring, left little. Use an inkpad with washable ink and ask everyone to make his or her fingerprints in the appropriate places. You may need to help the younger children in your family.

Thumbprint Cookies

You will need:
1 package Vanilla wafer cookies
⅔ cup clear Karo syrup
2 tablespoons vanilla
½ cup jelly or preserves

Place the vanilla wafers into a gallon-size baggie and seal it closed. Crush the cookies with your hands until they are tiny crumbs.

Place the cookie crumbs in a mixing bowl. Add the Karo syrup and vanilla. Mix well, using your hands.

Shape the dough into 1-inch balls and place them on a cookie sheet. Press your thumb to indent the center of the balls. Spoon jelly or preserves into the indentation. Cover and chill for one hour before serving.

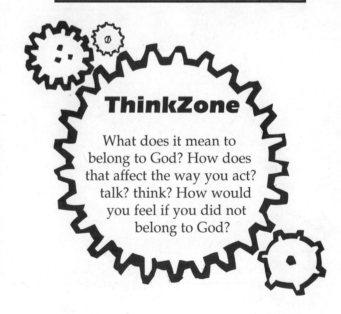

ThinkZone

What does it mean to belong to God? How does that affect the way you act? talk? think? How would you feel if you did not belong to God?

God made all people.

I Am Uniquely Me!

My name is _____

I am _____ years old.

No one has these
but me.

Reproducible 10D

BIBLEZONE®

He's Got the Whole World in His Hands

He's got the whole world in His hands
He's got the whole world in His hands
He's got the whole world in His hands
He's got the whole world in His hands

He's got the wind and the rain in His hands
He's got the wind and the rain in His hands
He's got the wind and the rain in His hands
He's got the whole world in His hands

He's got the tiny little baby in His hands
He's got the tiny little baby in His hands
He's got the tiny little baby in His hands
He's got the whole world in His hands

He's got you and me, brother, in His hands
He's got you and me, sister, in His hands
He's got you and me, brother, in His hands
He's got the whole world in His hands

He's got the whole world in His hands
He's got the whole world in His hands
He's got the whole world in His hands
He's got the whole world in his hands

Reproducible 10E

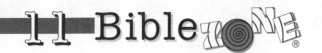

The Naming

Enter the

Bible Verse

God appointed human beings rulers over everything God had made.

Psalm 8:6, *Good News Bible*, adapted

Bible Story

Genesis 1:28-31; 2:19-20

God did not simply create and then move on. God created, provided, and gave human beings the task of being the caretakers over all that God had created.

When we hear the word *dominion* today, it is easy to think that God has given human beings the power and the authority to control. We often consider *dominion* and *domination* interchangeable. However, the word *dominion* means much more than that. *Dominion* means being responsible for something. In this case human beings are responsible for the care of God's world. We are to act as God's presence in the world. To have dominion means to protect and provide not only for our own needs, but also for the needs of everything that God created. God created human beings to be in partnership with God. As partners, humans have the responsibility of caring for God's earth and for God's creatures—including other humans. God created human beings to fulfill God's purposes for creation.

Children are close to their environments—both physically and spiritually. They look at the world with awe and wonder. Every-thing is a miracle—the birth of a baby bird, the first flowers of spring, the rainbow in the sky. They take the time to appreciate God's wonderful creation. They welcome the responsibility of caring for God's gift.

For this reason it is easy to motivate boys and girls to participate in environmental activities. Recycling programs have taken off because of children's involvement. The children seem to be more aware of what they will lose if the reckless abandon does not stop. But the children do not have power, except in their ability to motivate the adults around them.

There is a biblical and theological basis for care of the earth. Environmental protection is more than a law; it is God's command. God even entrusted human beings to name the animals. As we teach boys and girls how to care for God's gifts, we are training the future adults who will someday have the power, the resources, and the motivation to accomplish environmental reform.

God gave human beings the task of taking care of God's creation.

Scope the

ZONE	TIME	SUPPLIES	◎ ZILLIES®
Zoom Into the Zone			
Get in the Zone	5 minutes	page 174, cassette player	Cassette
Name That Thing	10 minutes	Reproducible 11D, markers	none
Wacky Name Game	10 minutes	none	ping pong ball, atom ball, earth kickball, creature kick-ball, plastic egg, fun loop straw, paper blow-out, bouncing rock ball, celestial ball
BibleZone®			
Zoom Into the Bible	15 minutes	Bible for each student	none
Enjoy the Story	15 minutes	Reproducibles 11A and 11B	none
Riddle Race	15 minutes	Reproducible 11C, trash can or box	ping pong balls
LifeZone			
Caretaker Checklist	15 minutes	Bible, large piece of paper, marker	none
Sing	5 minutes	Reproducible 11E, cassette player	Cassette
Praise	10 minutes	magazines, glue, large piece of paper, marker	none

◎ Zillies® are found in the **BibleZone® FUNspirational® Kit.**

Zoom Into the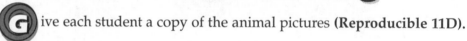

Choose one or more activities to catch your children's interest.

Supplies:
page 174,
cassette player

Zillies®:
Cassette

Get in the Zone

Have "The Bible Zone" **(Cassette)** playing as the students enter the room. Greet each student with a happy smile and **say: Welcome to the BibleZone!**

Give each student a a copy of the words to "The Bible Zone" **(page 174).** Play the song again and invite everyone to sing with you.

Supplies:
Reproducible 11D,
markers

Zillies®:
none

Name That Thing

Give each student a copy of the animal pictures **(Reproducible 11D).**

Ask: What do these animals look like?

Encourage the students to name the different parts they see on each animal. Invite them to use markers to add funny colors and marks on each animal.

Ask: What could we name these animals? *(Accept answers.)* **Why did you choose these names?**

Supplies:
none

Zillies®:
ping pong ball,
atom ball,
earth kickball,
creature kickball,
plastic egg,
fun loop straw,
paper blow-out,
bouncing rock
ball, celestial ball

Wacky Name Game

Ask: Why do you think we have names? What would happen if everyone had the same name?

Place a **ping pong ball, atom ball, earth kickball, creature kickball, plastic egg, fun loop straw, paper blow-out, bouncing rock ball,** and **celestial ball** on the table. Ask everyone to help you name the items.

Say: Let's find out how important it is to have a name. Let's each take a turn and ask for one item from the table. We will say, "Please give me a . . ." but no one can say the name of the item. *(Repeat the names.)* **Somehow you have to describe it so that we understand what you are asking for.**

Take turns. If anyone uses the name of the item, make a funny noise to signal he or she must begin again.

Choose one or more activities to immerse your children in the Bible story.

Zoom Into the Bible

Say: It is much easier to communicate when we know the name of the item or person we are talking about. Until something has a name, it is as though it does not really exist. In today's Bible story we go back to the beginning of God's creation, when not even the animals had names.

Be sure each student has a Bible. Ask everyone to read Genesis 1:28-31 and 2:19-20. **Ask:**
What did God give humans over every living thing? *(dominion)*
What does dominion mean? *(being responsible for something)*
What responsibility did God give Adam? *(naming all the creatures)*

Supplies:
Bible for each student

Zillies®:
none

Enjoy the Story

Tell or read the story "The Name Game" **(Reproducibles 11A and 11B).**
Ask: How difficult do you think it would be to name a creature?
What about every living creature?
What kind of responsibility do you think that was for Adam?
What kind of responsibility do you think that gives us?

Supplies:
Reproducibles 11A and 11B

Zillies®:
none

Riddle Race

Give each student a **ping pong ball**. Have everyone stand in a large, open circle with a box or trash can placed in the middle of the circle.

Say: I am going to say a riddle about an animal. When I finish, if you think you know the answer to the riddle, toss your ping pong ball into the container. The first person to get his or her ball in gets to answer.

Read the riddles **(Reproducible 11C)**, each time having the students toss the ping pong balls to determine who gets to answer.

Supplies:
Reproducible 11C, trash can or box

Zillies®:
ping pong balls

The Name Game

by Michael E. Williams

A long time ago, when the world was still new, none of the creatures had been named. It was very confusing because you couldn't tell one creature from another. Of course, they all looked different, but without names they had nothing to call each other or themselves.

To clear up the confusion God decided to have a contest to name the creatures. Any of them could venture a guess at a name if they wanted. There was great excitement in the garden on the day of the contest.

All of the creatures were lined up on one side of the garden. Each was asked one by one to step out of line, turn around and face the other creatures, and await his or her name.

God called for the elephant (who was not named that yet, of course) to step forward. Several animals attempted a name.

Duck suggested, "Large gray boulder with leaves for ears."

"It certainly is descriptive, but it seems a little clumsy," God replied.

"Hose nose," grumped the hippopotamus (who hadn't yet been named that, either).

"More like a nickname than a real name," said God.

"Just a bigger version of me," squeaked rat, who, even though he didn't have a name yet either, was very self-centered.

"No, that won't work," God responded quickly.

The earthling, the one creature that had been named—in fact, named Adam (which means "earthling")—spoke up. "How about elephant?" he said very matter of factly.

"It has a ring to it." God smiled, almost like the name tasted good on the tongue. "Short and simple. Elephant it shall be."

Then God asked the armadillo to step forward.

"Little armored friend who can roll up in a ball," spoke moose.

"Again, a little too long and cumbersome for easy use." It was clear God wanted to simplify whenever possible.

"Flank tank," suggested the hippo, who was proving to be something of a poet.

"Too easy to make fun of," God replied. "Besides, I don't get the flank part."

"It just sounded good," said hippo, unable to mask the disappointment in his voice.

"Road kill," sneered the opossum.

"You're a good one to talk," was God's only reply.

Again, the earthling spoke. "How about armadillo? It gets the armor part in there, while it still sounds like something that can curl up in a ball."

Reproducible 11A

BibleZone®

"Very good." God looked straight at Adam and continued, "You seem to have a knack for naming."

"Thanks," was Adam's only reply.

Then God called for the kangaroo to step out of line and face the crowd.

The deer thought that "deer that jumps around with its young in its pocket" would be good.

"We probably need to keep these names pretty simple, or we will never remember them. Appropriate but too long," God decided.

"Spring thing." Hippo was at it again.

"Short, descriptive, and it rhymes, but not quite right," God added quickly.

"How about marsupial?" The snake, who was considered very smart by almost everyone, was speaking now.

"It does have a scientific ring to it," God agreed, "but may serve better for a group rather than a single creature. Make a note. Let's remember that."

"Kangaroo?" ventured Adam.

"Where did you come up with that one?" God asked.

"I don't know," the earthling replied. "It just sounded as exotic as the creature looked."

"It works for me," God agreed. "Let's keep it."

In an attempt to be fair God called for an insect, the grasshopper, to step forward next.

"One who waits in the grass to surprise others," suggested the cat, who loved to chase after just such insects.

"Too long," God quipped, "though I like the reference to grass. That puts the creature in context."

"Hopper bopper," blurted out hippo, who had been thinking and not listening to God's last comment about liking the part about grass.

Before God could comment, though, Adam jumped in with, "Grasshopper! That would keep the best of both suggestions."

"Good," pondered God. "This is all very good."

As it turned out, the earthling, Adam, named the rest of the creatures, though he did incorporate suggestions from the others. And the snake added a few of the more difficult scientific names.

As a reward God offered Adam the choice of any of the creatures he had named to be a lifelong companion. "It's just not good for you to be alone," is the way God had phrased it.

"Don't get me wrong," Adam told God. "I'm grateful. And there are some awfully nice creatures here. I think I could be friends with them. But a lifelong companion is different. You want somebody very much like yourself for that."

"I understand," God told Adam.

Then God formed another earthling, one just right to be a companion so the two could live side by side from that time on.

And so we have.

Reproducible 11B

Animal Riddles

by LeeDell Stickler

This creature has four legs and a long bushy striped tail. Its body is covered with thick fur. It looks like a bandit because it is always wearing a mask. I think I will call it a _____. (raccoon)

This creature has four legs and lives in family groups called prides. It has a long mane and a very loud roar. I think I will call it a _____. (lion)

This creature has four legs and lives in the forests. It has thick fur and a long nose. It likes to eat honey and climb trees. I think I will call it a _____. (bear)

This creature has no legs at all, but it can move very fast. It eats small animals such as mice and lizards. It makes a rattling sound to warn you to "beware." I think I will call it a _____. (rattlesnake)

This creature has only two legs. Its body is covered with bright feathers—red, blue, green, and yellow. It lives high in the trees of the tropical rain forest. I think I will call it a _____. (parrot)

This creature has no legs at all and lives in the sea. It looks like a fish, but it has lungs and breathes air. This creature is one of the largest creatures God created. I think I will call it a _____. (whale)

This creature has four legs and carries its house around on its back. It eats leaves and bugs. It moves very slowly. I think I will call it a _____. (turtle)

This creature has four legs and lives on the plains. It has a very long neck so that it can reach the topmost leaves of trees. This creature has brown spots on its body. I think I will call it a _____. (giraffe)

This creature has eight legs and lives in the water. Its favorite home is in the ocean near a coral reef. This creature moves about by squirting jets of water. I think I will call it an _____. (octopus)

This creature also has eight legs, but it lives on the land. It spins a web, where it catches bugs for its dinner. I think I will call it a _____. (spider)

This creature has no legs at all but moves about just fine. Instead of breathing air this animal breathes water through its gills. It has fins and scales. I think I will call it a _____. (fish)

This creature has two legs and lives in caves and dark attics. It flies and is covered with fur. It makes a high-pitched squeaking sound to locate objects. It drinks the nectar of some plants and eats primarily insects. This creature sleeps during the day and flies around at night. I think I will call it a _____. (bat)

Caretaker Checklist

Supplies:
Bible, large piece of paper, marker

Zillies®:
none

(R) ead Genesis 1:26-30 to the class. **Ask: What did God give to human beings?** *(everything that God had created)* **What did God tell the human beings?** *(Be fruitful and multiply; fill the earth and have dominion over it.)*

Say: Dominion does not mean to have power over all the things of the earth. Dominion means to be responsible for all the things of the earth and to care for them and to protect them. God made us caretakers.

Write 1 to 10 across the top of a large piece of paper. **Say: Let's do a checklist and see how good we are as caretakers of God's creation. I will call out something we should do. You decide what your ranking is on each one—10 is great; 1 is really bad. Be honest as you choose the numbers to write.**

Say each of the following statements. Each time check the numbers the students call out.

1. I remember not to litter.
2. I recycle newspaper.
3. I turn off water while I brush my teeth or wash my face.
4. I save or recycle boxes.
5. I use both sides of drawing or writing paper.
6. I recycle glass bottles.
7. I recycle aluminum cans.
8. I turn off lights when I leave the room.
9. I do not waste food.
10. I take short showers.
11. I use paper towels, bathroom tissue, and facial tissue sparingly.
12. I treat all animals with respect.

When finished tally the score. Multiply 120 by the number of students in the room. (Be certain to include yourself if you included your responses.) **Say: Out of a possible _____, we scored _____.**

Encourage the students to think of ways they could be better caretakers of God's creation. Ask each person to name one thing he or she could do that would make a difference and help care for God's world.

 God gave human beings the task of taking care of God's creation.

Life Zone

Choose one or more activities to bring the Bible to life.

Supplies:
Reproducible 11E,
cassette player

Zillies®:
Cassette

Supplies:
magazines, glue,
large piece of
paper, marker

Zillies®:
none

Sing

(G)ive each student a copy of the words to the song "God's Wacky Animals" **(Reproducible 11E).** Play the song on the **Cassette** and ask everyone to follow along. Play the song again and invite everyone to sing with you.

Praise

(H)ave several pictures of creation—lakes or rivers, forests, grain fields, flowers, animals, industrial areas, city streets, neighborhoods, gardens, schools, fish, insects, and birds—cut out of magazines. Invite the students to tear uneven edges around each picture.

Say: God did not simply create and then move on. God created, provided for, and gave human beings the task of being the caretakers of all that God had created. Our Bible verse for today is adapted from Psalm 8:6 in the *Good News Bible:* "God appointed human beings rulers over everything God had made. "

Place a large piece of paper on the table. Ask one or more students to write today's verse on the paper. Then invite everyone to select pictures to glue onto the paper. Assure the students it is all right for the pictures to touch or overlap.

When the students are finished, **say: God has created a big, wonderful, beautiful world filled with incredible things. It is our job to take care of God's creation.**

Pray: Dear God, help us to be good caretakers of your great world. What we have messed up, help us to fix. Where we have not tried hard enough, help us to try harder. Help us to inspire others to care for your world too. Amen.

God gave human beings the task of taking care of God's creation.

Give each student a copy of HomeZone® to enjoy this week.

138

Environmental SOS

God's world could really use your help! You might be just one person, but you can ask your family and other families to join you to really make a difference. Here's a list of some groups that are already working to help. Write to them and get more information. They will write back. Many even have web sites so you can keep up with current news on the environment.

Center for Marine Conservation
1725 DeSales Street, NW
Washington, DC 20036

National Wildlife Federation
1412 Sixteenth St., NW
Washington, DC 20036

World Resources Institute
1735 New York Avenue
Washington, DC 20006

The Nature Conservancy International
1815 North Lynn Street
Suite 800
Arlington, VA 22209
(check your local chapter)

Renew America
1400 Sixteenth St., NW
Suite 700
Washington, DC 20036
(They keep a record of environmental successes!)

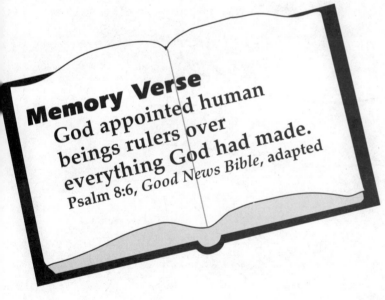

Memory Verse
God appointed human beings rulers over everything God had made.
Psalm 8:6, Good News Bible, adapted

ThinkZone
Why is it important for everyone to take his or her responsibility for God's creation seriously? What would the world be like if more people did? if fewer people did?

God gave human beings the task of taking care of God's creation.

Reproducible 11D

God's Wacky Animals

God's wacky animals
God's wacky animals

Do your dance, swing through the trees
Limb to limb, hang by your knees
Upside down, up in the outside
Grab a friend, slip down the downslide
Up again, dance on the ceiling
Raise the roof, show what you're feeling
Shake it up to the next level
Shout to God, sing it to heaven

Chorus:
God's wacky animals
God's wacky animals
The animal kingdom looks crazy
Goin' bananas, gettin' nuts
But God's wacky animals know what's up

Do your dance from the heart
Never ever stop once you start
Make some noise, don't be sneaky
Hug somebody cheek to cheeky
Share the life that you're given
Let yourself go, shed your skin
Do your dance, show your elation
Jump up and join in God's creation

Repeat Chorus

God's wacky animals
God's wacky animals
God's wacky animals
God's wacky animals
God's wacky animals

Reproducible 11E

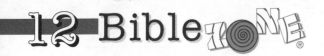

Trouble in Paradise

Enter the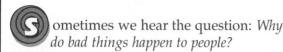

Bible Verse
You may eat the fruit of any tree in the garden, except the tree that gives knowledge of what is good and what is bad.

Genesis 2:16-17, *Good News Bible*

Bible Story
Genesis 3:1-24

Sometimes we hear the question: *Why do bad things happen to people?*

The story of Adam and Eve and the Tree of Life in the center of the Garden of Eden helped the early Hebrew people understand where evil came from. When God created human beings, God gave them the gift that God did not bestow on other living things—the ability to choose. Human beings could choose to do good or to do evil. Sin came into the world when human beings decided that instead of being subject to God, they wanted to be the same as God.

Human beings soon learned that along with the freedom to choose comes the responsibility for what happens as a result of the ability to make choices. One of those consequences was humans' awareness of their own sins. In spite of the harsh judgment that came as a result of their disobedience, God still showed compassion to prideful human beings.

As we read this story today, we begin to see the answer to an often-asked question: *Why does a loving God allow bad things to happen to us?* The answer lies somewhere in the role of

freedom of choice and its effect on our relationships with God and with one another.

As children get older, we want them to make more choices for themselves. But we want these choices to be good ones. Experience tells us that children will not always choose wisely. As parents or teachers it is instinctual for us to try to shield our children from the consequences of bad decisions. However, suffering the consequence of a poor choice can be an excellent teacher for a child. You as an adult can only hope to prevent the children from making life-threatening choices. Affirm them as children of God. Remind them that God loves and cares about them no matter what they do. God may not always like what they do, but God will always love them.

Note: There may be children in your class who have been or are currently being abused. They may wonder why God permits such atrocities. Children often become the innocent victims of the consequences of adult behavior. Be an advocate for your children. Let them know God's love through you.

ZONE IN

God wants us to choose what is right.

Scope the ZONE

ZONE	TIME	SUPPLIES	⊙ ZILLIES®
Zoom Into the Zone			
Get in the Zone	5 minutes	page 174, cassette player	Cassette
Pay Up!	15 minutes	Reproducible 12C, scissors, brown paper bag, masking tape, trash can	celestial ball
BibleZone®			
Zoom Into the Bible	20 minutes	Bible for each student	none
Enjoy the Story	15 minutes	Reproducibles 12A and 12B	none
LifeZone			
Blow It Out	15 minutes	white paper, brown and green tempera paint, recycled newspaper, small sponges, small bowls, resealable plastic bags, spoons	fun loop straws
Remember the Word	10 minutes	Reproducible 12D, markers	none
Sing	5 minutes	Reproducible 12E, cassette player	Cassette
Do Right Rap	5 minutes	none	none

⊙ Zillies® are found in the **BibleZone® FUNspirational® Kit.**

Zoom Into the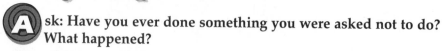

Choose one or more activities to catch your children's interest.

Supplies:
page 174,
cassette player

Zillies®:
Cassette

Supplies:
Reproducible 12C,
scissors, brown
paper bag,
masking tape,
trash can

Zillies®:
celestial ball

Get in the Zone

Have "The Bible Zone" **(Cassette)** playing as the students enter the room. Greet each student with a happy smile and **say: Welcome to the BibleZone!**

Have copies of the words **(page 174)** available if anyone needs them. Play the song again and invite everyone to sing with you.

Pay Up!

Ask: Have you ever done something you were asked not to do? What happened?

Invite the students to play a game about consequences. Cut out the consequence cards **(Reproducible 12C)** and put them in a brown paper bag. (Have enough copies that you have two cards for every student.) Place a trash can next to a wall. Use masking tape to mark a throw line several feet from the trash can.

Hold up the inflatable **celestial ball. Say: I want everyone to line up. One at a time, I want you to stand at the throw line and throw the ball into the trash can. If you miss, you will have to pay the consequences.**

As each student misses the trash can, have him or her draw a consequence card out of the bag and do what the card says. Continue play until everyone has drawn from the bag twice.

Say: In today's Bible story we are going to learn more about Adam and Eve. We remember that God had created the wonderful Garden of Eden where they could live. God had provided everything they needed. God had asked only one thing of Adam and Eve. Does anyone remember what that was? (not to eat from the tree of the knowledge of good and evil) **But what happened?** (The serpent convinced Eve to eat, and she convinced Adam to eat from the tree.) **There were consequences as the result of their decision to eat from the tree. Today we are going to find out what those consequences were.**

 God wants us to choose what is right.

Choose one or more activities to immerse your children in the Bible story.

Zoom Into the Bible

Supplies:
Bible for each student

Zillies®:
none

(B)e certain each student has a Bible. Divide the students into four teams. Ask Team One to read Genesis 3:1-7; Team Two to read Genesis 3:8-13; Team Three to read Genesis 3:14-19; and Team Four to read Genesis 3:20-24.

Ask Team One:
What did God ask Eve not to do? *(eat from the tree in the middle of the garden, or even touch the tree)*
What did God say the consequences would be if they ate from the tree or touched it? *(They would die.)*
How did the serpent tempt Eve? *(told her she would be like God if she ate from the tree; she would know good and evil)*
What did Eve do? *(ate some of the fruit and gave some to Adam)*
What did Adam do? *(ate the fruit)*
What happened to them? *(They became ashamed and made clothes for themselves from fig leaves.)*

Ask Team Two:
What did Adam and Eve try to do? *(hide from God)*
How did Adam explain eating the fruit? *(He blamed Eve.)*
How did Eve explain eating the fruit? *(The serpent tricked her.)*

Ask Team Three:
What did God do to the serpent? *(The serpent would always crawl on the ground and be the enemy of humans.)*
What did God do to Eve? *(made childbirth painful and made her husband rule over her)*
What did God do to Adam? *(would always have to work hard until he died)*

Ask Team Four:
What did God do to Adam and Eve? *(sent them out of the garden)*
What did God use to guard the tree of life? *(an angel and flaming sword)*

Enjoy the Story

Supplies:
Reproducibles 12A and 12B

Zillies®:
none

(T)ell or read the story "A Love Letter From God" **(Reproducibles 12A and 12B). Ask:**
How do you think God felt when Adam and Eve disobeyed God?
How do you think God feels when you disobey God?
What do you think hurts God the most?

A Love Letter From God

by Michael E. Williams

ear Adam and Eve:

It breaks my heart to write this letter to you, but there are some things I need to tell you before you leave the garden forever. First of all, you are my beloved children and always will be. Never forget that. You may forget many things that happened here, but do not forget that I love you. I will remind you whenever I can.

You were created so I would have someone like me to love. You were to be someone who could be creative. After all you named the other creatures, with my help, of course. You were to learn to laugh and to tell stories and to do all those other things that made you like me. You were created so I would not be lonely, and you were created for each other so you both would not be lonely either. You were created so we could be as close to each other as each other's skins, as each other's breath. That will never be the same again.

I only wanted the best for you, and I thought I could provide it for you. You wouldn't have to make any decisions. Everything would be provided for you. And you would have your freedom. If you were not free, then you couldn't really be like me.

That was the reason for the tree in the middle of the garden. You had to have the freedom to make the choice of whether or not to eat from that tree. It held the knowledge of good and evil, between which you really didn't want the responsibility of choosing. I wanted to do that for you so you

would only know the good things of life. I suppose all parents want that for their children. Still, you had to have the freedom to choose for yourselves.

Then there was the serpent. He is a prime example of the saying that a little learning is a dangerous thing. While he was the smartest creature in the garden, he outsmarted himself. He thought he was laying a trap for you when, in fact, the trap would catch him, as well. This is what we call justice, but you don't know about that yet.

When I came into the garden and you were hiding, I knew in my heart of hearts what had happened. Then when you told me you knew you were naked, there was no question what had happened. You had eaten from the tree I had warned you about. I thought I would be angry if that ever happened. Instead, I was shattered. I wanted to weep. My heart broke for me, and for you, and for your children and their children and all the generations down through the ages. They would never know what it was like to live here, how beautiful and easy life was. They would know the story of how it was lost, that's all.

If only you had been able to realize that you are like me already in every way that counts. Then when the serpent tempted you by saying you would be like God, you could have said, "We already are!" The only part of my image you didn't have to bear was the burden of responsibility. You didn't have to make decisions and live with their consequences. That was all up to me.

Reproducible 12A

BibleZone®

Now you will have to bear those burdens, though. Knowing good and evil you will be forced to choose between the two. And the way between them is not always clear, and the choices are rarely easy. You will have to rise with the sun and work all day just so you can live. You will love your children as I have loved you, only to see them grow up and break your heart. You will live in fear of the serpent and try to kill him. He will live in fear of you, and his bite will be deadly to you.

You and your children will have to do many things that you don't want to do. You will be assigned homework, and it will seem never to be finished. The things that are most healthy for you will be the things you don't want to eat. On the other hand the things you most love, chocolate and cheeseburgers, will be bad for you.

And you will die. I know you thought that you would fall down dead as soon as you took a bite of the fruit. That would have been too easy. No, your dying will take a whole lifetime.

You have no idea what you have done. Or what I could have done for you had you remained my little children. Now you will have to grow up, and there are only certain things I can do for you. I gifted you with freedom, so there are many things you will have to do for yourself. You will have to take care of each other, the other creatures, and the earth. I will help you, but I will no longer be able to do it for you. You will have to listen to each other, the other creatures, and the earth. You will have to

hear when another is in pain and not close your ears to the cry. Then it will be up to you to respond. And you must listen to me.

You will learn the ways of the world, but I will be there to teach you my ways too. You must live in the world but not let the world shape what you think and do. Allow my love and my words to you to shape what you think and do. I will be there to whisper in your ear and to nudge you in the right direction. All you will need to do is listen and follow as best you can.

Now come to me and take these gifts I have for you. Your poorly made fig leaf clothes are rough and scratchy. Since I do not want my children to be too uncomfortable, I have made you clothing from the softest of skins to wear. When you wear these clothes, remember that I made them with my own hand just for you. That's how much I care for you.

Go now. Though you may travel far from me, I will never be far from you. You need never be alone or afraid, though you may feel that way sometimes. Even then I will be with you. And when it comes your time to die, you will not disappear into nothing-ness. I will be there to receive you in my arms, to embrace you and to welcome you home. For, you see, home will always be where I am.

Love,

God

Reproducible 12B

147

Hop up and down on one foot around the room.	Put your elbow to your knee. Hop around in a circle.	Make the silliest face you can think of.
Push a pencil across the room with your nose.	Hold an earth kickball between your knees and hop.	Balance a bouncing rock ball on your head and walk in a circle.
Walk around the room backwards.	Sing "Mary Had a Little Lamb."	Quack and walk like a duck.
Act like a ballerina.	Crab walk across the room.	Tell of your undying love for someone in the room.

Reproducible 12C

BibleZone®

Choose one or more activities to bring the Bible to life.

Blow It Out

(A) sk: What do you think the forbidden tree looked like in the center of the garden? What do you think the fruit looked like? The Bible doesn't identify the tree so that we can tell. Today we are going to imagine what we think the tree might have looked like.

Cover the tables with recycled newspaper. Give each student a sheet of white paper and a **fun loop straw.** (The fun loop straws should be stored in separate resealable plastic bags with the students' names written on the bags.) Place a dollop of brown paint on each paper.

Say: Use the straw to blow (do not use suction) the brown paint on the paper to create a tree with spidery looking branches.

When the branches are dry, have the students take bits of sponge and tempera paint to create the leaves and the fruit.

Say: God gave Adam and Eve the freedom to choose to do right or to do wrong. God could have prevented them from eating the fruit, but God wanted them to choose not to eat it. The story of Adam and Eve helps to explain to people how we go wrong. Whenever we try to be God instead of living as God wants us to live, then we choose wrong. When Adam and Eve ate from the forbidden tree, they didn't think of the consequences.

Ask: Where do you think Adam and Eve went? How do you think their lives changed? How do our lives change when we disobey God?

Say: Whenever we do wrong, there are always consequences.

Remember the Word

(G) ive each student a photocopy of today's Bible verse (**Reproducible 12D**). Ask everyone to read the verse with you.

Invite everyone to use markers to add color to the drawings. While everyone is working, **ask: What do you think would have happened if Adam and Eve had made the right choice? What do you think happens when we make the right choices?**

Supplies:
white paper, brown and green tempera paint, recycled newspaper, small sponges, small bowls, resealable plastic bags, spoons

Zillies®:
fun loop straws

Supplies:
Reproducible 12D, markers

Zillies®:

Choose one or more activities to bring the Bible to life.

Supplies:
Reproducible 12E,
cassette player

Zillies®:
Cassette

Sing

 ive each student a copy of the words to the song "He's Got the Whole World in His Hands" **(Reproducible 12E).** Play the song on the **Cassette** and ask the students to follow along. Play the song again and invite everyone to sing with you.

Supplies:
none

Zillies®:
none

Do Right Rap

 each the boys and girls the response to the "Do Right Rap." Give it a beat and encourage everyone to have fun.

Response: I want to do what's right.
Uh huh, uh huh.
I want to follow God's way.
Uh huh, uh huh.

Say:
I want to follow God's way in everything I do.
Don't want nobody saying I don't know how to choose.
Response
Don't want no one to look at me and see someone who's bad.
I want to follow God's way, don't want God to be sad.
Response
The Bible tells me how to live; it puts me to the test.
I want to follow God's way, 'cause that's the way that's best.
Response

Pray: Dear God, thank you for your wonderful creation. Thank you for giving us the ability to make choices. Help us to make choices wisely so we may do what is right for you and for all human beings. Amen.

 God wants us to choose what is right.

Give each student a copy of HomeZone® to enjoy this week.

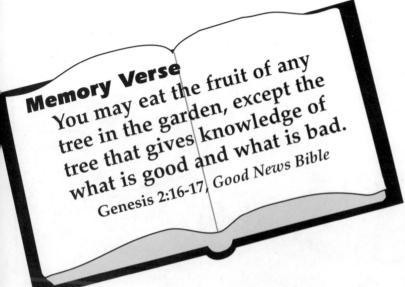

Memory Verse

You may eat the fruit of any tree in the garden, except the tree that gives knowledge of what is good and what is bad.

Genesis 2:16-17, *Good News Bible*

Snake Stuff

Did you know that snakes are a gardener's best friend? Most snakes love to eat rodents and other pests that destroy gardens.

Some people think a snake's skin is slimy feeling, but it isn't. It is cool and dry!

Did you know the anaconda is the biggest and heaviest snake in the world? It can grow up to thirty feet long and may weigh up to six hundred pounds.

Did you know the hog-nosed snake (a non-poisonous snake) plays dead when startled by an enemy? First it twists and turns as if it is in pain; then it rolls over and plays dead.

Fried Snakes

You will need:
1 (5-ounce) can chow mein noodles
1 (3-ounce) can chow mein noodles
1 (12-ounce) package chocolate chips
1 (12-ounce) package butterscotch chips

Melt the chocolate chips and the butterscotch chips together in the top of a double boiler. Stir them together. Remove the pan from the double boiler. Carefully stir in both cans of chow mein noodles.

Drop the mixture by spoonfuls onto wax paper to cool.

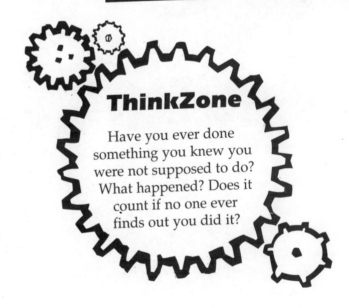

ThinkZone

Have you ever done something you knew you were not supposed to do? What happened? Does it count if no one ever finds out you did it?

God wants us to choose what is right.

151

You may eat the fruit of any tree in the garden,

except the tree that gives knowledge of what is good and what is bad.

(GENESIS 2:16-17, GOOD NEWS BIBLE)

152

Reproducible 12D

BIBLEZONE®

He's Got the Whole World in His Hands

He's got the whole world in His hands
He's got the whole world in His hands
He's got the whole world in His hands
He's got the whole world in His hands

He's got the wind and the rain in His hands
He's got the wind and the rain in His hands
He's got the wind and the rain in His hands
He's got the whole world in His hands

He's got the tiny little baby in His hands
He's got the tiny little baby in His hands
He's got the tiny little baby in His hands
He's got the whole world in His hands

He's got you and me, brother, in His hands
He's got you and me, sister, in His hands
He's got you and me, brother, in His hands
He's got the whole world in His hands

He's got the whole world in His hands
He's got the whole world in His hands
He's got the whole world in His hands
He's got the whole world in his hands

A Season for Everything

Enter the

Bible Verse

For everything there is a season,
and a time for every matter under heaven.
Ecclesiastes 3:1

Bible Story

Ecclesiastes 3:1-8

God did not create a temporary, static world. Growth, change, and renewal are a part of God's plan. Seeds are a part of every plant. God told the animals and people to "be fruitful and multiply." God built in the means for a continuing creation. Without this natural process, through which the earth and all that is in it continue to reproduce, life as we know it could not exist.

Song of Solomon, Ecclesiastes, and Psalms celebrate this time of planned renewal—the growing season of spring that comes after the rainy winter, and the rich blessings of each of the seasons. As human beings we are not able to understand the complexity of God's plan for creation, but how reassuring to know that God is definitely in charge!

Growth and change are concepts intimately related to the older elementary child. Their bodies are a constant source of amazement to them, as they are experiencing rapid physical and emotional changes. Their growing takes a lot of energy, sometimes leaving them lethargic. But what is most confusing to them is that there are great variations of emotional and physical growth among older elementary-age students. They are different from one another and different from who they were just a short time ago.

Children grow on the inside too. They learn new things from year to year. Children are, however, often puzzled as to why they have to learn certain things. Older elementary boys and girls are able to project into a future time, but they still depend upon adults to determine what skills they need to learn and when. We have to keep in mind, however, that a child who is not ready for a particular concept *will not grasp it*. God has a plan, and we all grow into it.

Another issue of growing and changing has to do with death. Most children have experienced death—either in the death of a pet, a relative, or a friend. Death is a part of life. All living things die. Deal with death in a sensitive and caring manner. Let the maturity level of the children guide answers to any questions they may ask on this subject.

God has a plan for all creation.

Scope the ZONE

ZONE	TIME	SUPPLIES	ZILLIES
Zoom Into the Zone			
Get in the Zone	5 minutes	page 174, cassette player	Cassette
Time's Up	10 minutes	resealable plastic bags (one per student)	ping pong balls, paper blow-outs
BibleZone®			
Opposites Attract	10 minutes	red and blue markers, index cards, basket	none
Zoom Into the Bible	15 minutes	Bible for each student	none
LifeZone			
Enjoy the Story	15 minutes	Reproducibles 13A and 13B	none
Month-to-Month Bible Verses	20 minutes	Reproducible 13D, several Bibles, concordance, scissors, stapler and staples, markers, pens, various kinds of decorative paper	none
Sing	5 minutes	Reproducible 13E, cassette player	Cassette
Praise	5 minutes	Reproducible 13C, scissors, tape	yarn

Zillies® are found in the **BibleZone® FUNspirational® Kit.**

Zoom Into the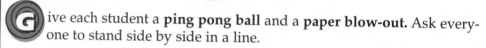

Choose one or more activities to catch your children's interest.

Supplies:
page 174,
cassette player

Zillies®:
Cassette

Get in the Zone

Have "The Bible Zone" **(Cassette)** playing as the students enter the room. Greet each student with a happy smile and **say: Welcome to the BibleZone!**

Have copies of the words **(page 174)** available if anyone needs them. Play the song again and invite everyone to sing with you.

Supplies:
resealable plastic
bags (one per
student)

Zillies®:
ping pong balls,
paper blow-outs

Time's Up!

Give each student a **ping pong ball** and a **paper blow-out.** Ask everyone to stand side by side in a line.

Say: When I say, "It's time to go!", everyone get on your hands and knees and place your ping pong ball on the floor in front of you. Use your paper blow-outs to blow the ping pong balls across the room. When you reach the other side of the room, turn around and blow your ping pong balls back to this side of the room. Remember, you can only move the ping pong balls by blowing on them. No touching with your hands! Keep blowing until I say, "Time's up!"

Continue play until some of the students have returned almost all the way back across the room, and then call out, "Time's up!" (Collect the paper blow-outs and put them in individual resealable plastic bags labeled with each student's name.)

Ask: What did you think when I called out, "Time's up?"
What happens when time is up? (*Something changes.*)

Say: The Bible tells us some very important things about time. The Bible tells us that God has a plan, a time, for everything!

God has a plan for all creation.

Opposites Attract

Supplies:
red and blue markers, index cards, basket

Zillies®:
none

(D) ivide the students into two teams. Explain that the two teams will compete against each other in a game of opposites.

Use a red marker to write each of the following words on index cards: *summer, up, over, hot, big, tall, open, forward, heavy, dark, smart, fast.* Place these cards in a basket.

Use a blue marker to write each of these words on index cards (prepare two sets of these words): *winter, down, under, cold, small, short, close, backward, light, light, stupid, slow.* Put one set face up on a table for each team.

Draw a card from the basket and present the words alternately to each team. See which teams select the opposite word first.

When all the cards have been played, **say: Much of life is filled with opposites. But God gave a time for all things.**

Zoom Into the Bible

Supplies:
Bible for each student

Zillies®:
none

(A) sk the students to remain in their teams. Be certain each student has a Bible. Ask the students to find the table of contents in the front of their Bibles.

Ask: In which testament do we find a book called Ecclesiastes? *(Old)*

Ask the students to find Ecclesiastes 3:1-8 in their Bibles.

Say: In these Scriptures we find opposites; for example, "a time to be born, and a time to die." I will read the first verse. Then, beginning with the second verse, I want the teams to alternate reading in unison the first part and the second part of each one.

Cue the teams as necessary.

Say: The Book of Ecclesiastes was written by a philosopher who was described as King David's son. In Ecclesiastes he looks back over the experiences of his life.

There Is a Season

by Michael E. Williams

School had started, and the weather was already beginning to get cool when Papa came to live with Eilene's family. Papa was Eilene's mother's father and was called "Papa" because that was how Eilene pronounced Grandpa when she was a baby. Eilene was his only grandchild. Since Eilene had never known her own father, Papa had been both a grandfather and father to her.

Until Papa moved in with them, Eilene's family had just included her mother, herself, and their cat named Boots. The cat was named for the four black swatches of hair that covered her lower legs and feet. Eilene had named her too.

By the time Papa had moved from his apartment a few blocks away to their apartment, he was very sick. His doctor had said it was cancer and that they would do everything they could. The surgeon said they felt the surgery was successful, but they did want to follow up with radiation and chemotherapy.

Papa was in the hospital over the Christmas holidays. Eilene and her mother took presents to his hospital room on Christmas Day; then he came to their house two days later. Eilene saw to it that his every need was met. In turn, he gave his granddaughter a travel mug they had given him in the hospital. It was a white cup with a bright red snap on top. On the side of the cup was a winter scene that looked like it was set somewhere in the country in New England. There was a house and a barn with a sleigh and lots of snow. In one corner of the winter scene it said, "Seasons Greetings." It was her most prized possession. She drank from it at every meal.

Something was bothering Eilene, and it showed on her face. When her Papa asked what was wrong, she hesitated to tell him right away. After a while, though, she blurted out, "Papa, are you going to die? I don't want you to die."

"Yes, I'm going to die, but no one knows exactly when. Believe me, I don't particularly want to die. It's just that dying is a part of life. Your grandmother died before you were born. I didn't want her to die, but the time came when she was too sick to go on living."

"Does everything die, Papa?" Eilene asked.

"Everything that lives does," Papa explained. "Dying just goes along with living. Just like in the fall the leaves on the trees turn red and yellow and then brown and finally fall to the ground. That's the season of their dying. After that everything seems dead. Then the snow falls and covers them with a beautiful white blanket. Then in the spring they come back again in a new form.

"People come to a season of dying too. It's just that our springtime is in a different world on the other side of death. We don't know exactly what that new life is going to be like, but it must be pretty good, since God prepared it for us."

Eilene clearly wasn't satisfied. "But why do people have to die?"

Reproducible 13A

Papa's calm voice seemed to wrap itself around her as he said, "Let me tell you a story. A long time ago there was an old king. As he came closer to the season of his own death, he started thinking back over his life. He had been very rich and powerful. He had been able to buy absolutely anything he wanted. He had been able to attend the best schools. He had gone to the best parties with the prettiest girls. The world had been at his fingertips.

"The king had also known the dark and difficult side of life, because he writes about that too. He had done foolish things, as we all have. He hadn't always made the best use of all that he had been given.

"When it came time for him to write down the wisdom he had gotten from all his living, he wrote, 'For everything there is a season and a time for everything that happens under heaven.'

"Then he goes through all the different things that can happen to a person during life; planting and harvesting, crying and drying tears, speaking and being quiet, losing and finding, grieving and dancing, and a lot more. He covers just about everything that goes on in life.

"Do you know what he begins with?" Papa paused for just a second and then said, "'A time to be born and a time to die.'

"He doesn't try to explain why there are these seasons in life, just that they are a part of life and always will be. It seems he thinks that 'Why?' is the wrong question."

"What is the right question?" Eilene sounded puzzled.

"If birth and death are all a part of life, then how are we supposed to live in between?

That's the only important question. And we can take part in creating the answer. You see, that's how we are like God—we're creative too. Maybe that's what it means to be in the image of God—to be creative. We can make choices about how we are going to live our lives. If we don't live well, we might as well be dead anyway.

"So the only question I have to answer is, 'How am I going to live between now and when I die?' And you can help me answer that. You can help me make good decisions."

Eilene was still sad at the idea that Papa would die, but she wasn't afraid to ask him questions about it anymore. He told her about when he had been a little boy and a young man. She asked if she could turn on her tape recorder so she could record all of his stories. She didn't want to forget any of them. He told her what he had asked the pastor at their church to include in his funeral, and asked Eilene if she approved. She did.

Then he asked what she thought should be written on the headstone that would be placed on the grave. She told Papa that she would have to think about that. At first she thought about "The World's Best Grandfather." Then she realized that only she would really understand what that meant, being his only granddaughter.

After lots of thinking she came up with the perfect idea. She ran into the room where her Papa lay on the hospital bed that had been brought in for him.

"I've got it," she proclaimed. "I know what should be written on your headstone."

"What is it?" her grandfather asked.

"For Everything There Is A Season."

159

Reproducible 13C

Permission granted to photocopy for local church use. © 1999 Abingdon Press.

BibleZone®

Choose one or more activities to bring the Bible to life.

Enjoy the Story

ell or read the story "There Is a Season" **(Reproducibles 13A and 13B).**

Ask: What did Papa mean about a season of dying and the springtime that comes after death?
What was the most important question for Papa? *(not when he would die, but how he would live between now and the time of his death)*

Invite the students to talk about pets, friends, or family members who have died. Be sensitive to their feelings and allow them to talk freely.

Month-to-Month Bible Verses

ave several copies of the Bible verse cards **(Reproducible 13D)** made and cut apart.

Ask: What are some of your favorite Bible verses?

Say: Let's select verses we want to remember all year, one for each month. Look at the Bible verse cards. Which seasons do they remind you of? Which cards are most like our seasons where we live?

Ask every student to select twelve cards. Help the students as needed to select the verses they want to remember. Have a concordance and several Bibles available.

When all of the verses have been selected and recorded, invite the students to make a cover for their Bible verse books. Have various kinds of paper to choose from—heavy wrapping paper, construction paper, recycled gift bags, decorative napkins. Have everyone staple the pages and covers together to keep.

 God has a plan for all creation.

Supplies:
Reproducibles 13A and 13B

Zillies®:
none

Supplies:
Reproducible 13D, several Bibles, concordance, scissors, stapler and staples, markers, pens, various kinds of decorative paper

Zillies®:

Choose one or more activities to bring the Bible to life.

Supplies:
Reproducible 13E,
cassette player

Zillies®:
Cassette

Supplies:
Reproducible 13C,
scissors, tape

Zillies®:
yarn

Sing

Give each student a copy of the words to the song "Your Wondrous Ways" **(Reproducible 13E)**. Play the song on the **Cassette** and ask the students to follow along. Play the song again and invite everyone to sing with you.

Praise

Photocopy the seasons cards **(Reproducible 13C)**. Spread the cards out face down and let each student select one. Then have the students tape their cards to the front of their clothes. Also select one for you to wear.

Have the students stand in a circle. Hold a ball of **yarn** in your hand.

Say: Each of us is wearing a card that shows a certain season. I will think about the card I am wearing, name the season—fall, winter, spring, or summer—and name something I am thankful for that is related to that season. Then I will hold the end of the yarn with one hand, and with the other hand, toss the ball to someone across the circle. Whoever catches the yarn should then name the season and name something he or she is thankful for related to the season shown on the card he or she is wearing. Then hold the yarn with one hand and use your other hand to toss the ball of yarn to someone else. We will continue until everyone has had an opportunity to speak.

Ask everyone to hold onto the web of yarn that has been created. **Say: God has created an orderly world with dependable cycles. The cycles of the seasons remind us that we also have cycles or seasons in our own lives. We experience sadness and happiness, active times and quiet times, wide-awake times and sleeping times. We all experience birth, and we all experience death. No matter what point we are at in our lives, we are always God's beloved children. We know that God has a plan for all creation, and we are a part of that plan.**

Pray: Thank you, God, for your plan of creation. We know that you will always be with us and love us. Amen.

Give each student a copy of HomeZone® to enjoy this week.

162

Memory Verse

For everything there is a season, and a time for every matter under heaven.

Ecclesiastes 3:1

Bird Table

You can be part of the wonderful balance of nature that God has created. Make a bird table!

Take an old cookie sheet and punch a hole at each corner. Punch several more small holes in the bottom of the pan so that rainwater will drain.

Thread one cord through the two corner holes in one end of the tray. Tie knots in both ends of the cord. Do the same thing with another cord through the two corner holes in the other end of the tray.

Hang the tray on a branch. Put food such as dried bread, apples cores, and bird seed on the bird table. Watch from a distance to see the birds enjoy dining at their table!

Timeless Cookies

You will need:
2 egg whites
⅔ cup sugar
pinch of salt
1 cup chocolate chips
¾ cup chopped nuts
1 teaspoon vanilla

Preheat your oven to 350 degrees.

Beat egg whites until stiff. Beat in sugar and salt. Fold in vanilla, chocolate chips, and nuts. Drop onto a greased cookie sheet or a cookie sheet covered with aluminum foil.

Put into the preheated oven. Turn off the oven and forget the cookies until morning! (Or until the oven has cooled to room temperature!)

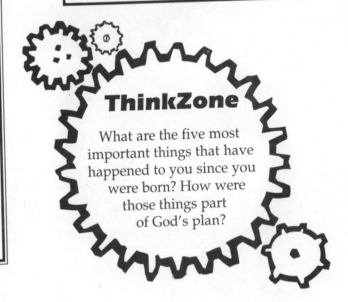

ThinkZone

What are the five most important things that have happened to you since you were born? How were those things part of God's plan?

God has a plan for all creation.

For everything
there is a season...
Month: _____
Bible Verse: _____
_____

For everything
there is a season...
Month: _____
Bible Verse: _____
_____

For everything
there is a season...
Month: _____
Bible Verse: _____
_____

For everything
there is a season...
Month: _____
Bible Verse: _____
_____

164

Reproducible 13D

BIBLEZONE®

Your Wondrous Ways

Ev'ry tiny grain of sand fashioned by Your loving hand
speaks of the marvelous mystery of Your plan.
Ev'ry star that lights the night, ev'ry flock of birds in flight
speaks of the splendor and joy of Your pow'r and might.

Oh Lord, Your wondrous ways are worthy of our praise.
Let all creation raise its voice and sing!
Let ev'ry tongue proclaim, Your name above all names.
You are Jehovah God our Lord and King.

Ev'ry dawn that greets the day with the sunshine's golden rays
speaks of the glorious miracles You have made.
Ev'ry drop of morning dew, ev'ry summer sky of blue
speaks of the beauty and wonder we find in You.

Oh Lord, Your wondrous ways, are worthy of our praise.
Let all creation raise its voice and sing!
Let ev'ry tongue proclaim, Your name above all names.
You are Jehovah God our Lord and King.
You are Jehovah God our Lord and King.

Writer: Janet McMahan-Wilson
Copyright © 1992 New Spring Publishing/ASCAP
All Rights Reserved.
Used by permission of Brentwood-Benson Music Publishing, Inc.
From the Brentwood-Benson Music Publishing, Inc. recording *God's Way A Song A Day, vol. 2*.

Reproducible 13E

Go Bowling

Divide the students into teams. Place a chair at one side of the room. Have members of the teams stand on the opposite side of the room and take turns trying to roll the **celestial ball** through the legs of the chair without touching any of the legs.

The team scores one point for a correct roll. If the ball touches a leg of the chair, a member of the opposing team can ask a question about today's lesson. The first team must answer the question correctly, or lose a turn.

Bird, Beast, or Fish

Choose one student to be the creator and to come to the front of the room. Have him or her throw a ping pong ball to another student.

As soon as the ball leaves the creator's hands, the creator calls out one of the three categories—bird, beast, or fish—and counts to six. Before the count reaches six, the student who catches the ball must name a creature fitting that category.

If the student succeeds, he or she throws the ball and names the category. If not, the creator at the front of the class throws again. Occasionally change categories to animal, vegetable, and mineral.

166

What a Team

Every lesson suggests that the students be divided into teams. You can use a variety of methods to create teams. That way the students are not bored, and they are not always on the same team!

Try some of these suggestions:
1. Divide by birthdays. The first six students born in the calendar year are on one team, the next six are on another team.

2. Put all the students' names in a paper bag. Draw out two names. Those students become the Team Leaders. Let them take turns drawing names until everyone is on a team.

3. Have the students line up in order by height. Select every other student to be on the same team.

4. Have the students line up in alphabetical order of their first names. Divide the line in half.

Fruit Salad Tag

Let each student choose the name of a fruit. If you have a large group, it is OK to have more than one student with the same fruit.

Set out a blanket or sheet at one end of the room. Indicate a starting line at the opposite end of the room. Select one student to be THE CHEF.

Say: Everyone must begin behind the starting line. The blanket is the salad bowl. THE CHEF is going to make a fruit salad. THE CHEF will call out the names of the various fruits he/she wants in the salad. The fruits named will try to get to the fruit bowl before THE CHEF tags them.

Anyone who is tagged gets to help THE CHEF on the next bowl of fruit salad. Continue playing until all the fruits have been tagged. The last fruit tagged becomes the next CHEF.

Mini Mobile

Hearty snacks can really move a group to action.

Scoop out the top center of a hotdog bun. Push a plastic drinking straw through the front and back of the bun to make holes for the axles. Poke the straw through the centers of four small rice-cake wheels. Slide two thin carrot sticks through the holes in the bun for axles. Attach the rice cake wheels. Attach halved olives for the headlights with toothpicks. Be sure to remove the tooth-picks before eating.

Fill the bun with your favorite sandwich filling and top it with a pretzel for a steer-ing wheel. Hold onto your hats!

Glorious Food

Food is always a way to involve students. If you have an after-school group or an evening session, let the boys and girls make some of these neat snacks.

Fruited Slushes

Want a way to cool off your cool group? Let them make exotic rainbow-colored fruit slushes.

Freeze assorted fruit juices in sepa-rate paper cups. Remove one frozen juice from its paper cup and place it in a plastic bag. Crush the juice into small pieces with the side of a wooden meat hammer. Repeat with each flavor of juice, keeping the pieces frozen until all the juices are crushed. Just before serving, spoon different-colored layers of the crushed juices into clear tall glasses.

The Real Nitty Gritty

 aint with colored sand. First sift and clean the sand. Mix water and several drops of food coloring in a jar. Add more coloring for a deeper tone.

Add the sand. Stir the mixture until the sand is evenly colored. Allow the sand to sit in the colored water for at least 15 minutes. Then carefully pour through a sieve.

Spread the sand out to dry on newspaper. When dry, pour the colored sand into a container. Keep the colors separate.

Draw a picture, leaving big areas blank. Paint those areas with white glue. Sprinkle the colored sand in those spaces. Allow to dry between colors.

Good Impressions

reate a dough from coffee grounds.

Coffee Dough:
1 cup flour
½ cup salt
1 cup coffee grounds
½ cup cold, leftover coffee

Mix ingredients together until blended. Gather mixture with your hands. Knead on a floured surface until you have a smooth dough. Store dough in a plastic bag or margarine tub.

Roll the dough about ½-inch thick. Cut the dough in any shape you want. Press special objects into the dough. Remove the objects. Make a hole in the top of the slab. Allow the dough to dry.

Make the Bible the Book They Love

Welcome to BibleZone®! These lessons are written especially to help the Bible become the book your students love the most. There are many things you can do to open the Bible to children. Many of the lessons have simple suggestions of things to do that will help your students build Bible skills. We want the message of the Bible to speak to children so they can live in response to the good news they find in the Scriptures.

Each week there is a memory verse for the students to learn. Memorizing Bible verses is an important skill for older elementary children to acquire. However, memorization can become a threat to their self-esteem unless cooperative memorization techniques are used. Instead of asking for individuals to recite in front of others, use a team approach in which the students help one another. Reinforce memorization in fun ways—in a song, through art projects, by playing games, or acting out the verses. Help them learn long passages by breaking them into shorter phrases and assigning phrases to teams. Have teams say their phrases in order to repeat the verses. If you have written phrases on index cards, swap the cards around for the teams to learn new phrases. Continue swapping the cards until everyone has learned the verse.

BibleZone® is fun! But in the midst of the fun there will be some serious learning happening! Make your own personal goals as you teach to help your students

- recognize the Bible as a revelation of God and a record of how people have experienced God;
- explore the meaning of Bible stories;
- learn the names of all the books of the Bible;
- learn how the Bible came to be;
- know that there are many translations and versions of the Bible;
- recognize sections of the Bible: Law, History, Poetry and Songs, Prophets, Gospels, Letters;
- learn to use tools such as a concordance, an atlas, and a Bible dictionary;
- explore stories in historical context;
- recognize the important role the Bible has had throughout history;
- recognize the Bible as the source of some worship resources used in their church;
- know that the Bible was written by many people over a long period of time;
- grow in their understanding of the relationship between the Bible message and their own relationship with God.

Enter the Story Zone

by Dr. Michael Williams

So you think you're not a storyteller. When was the last time someone asked you about a recent trip! What did you tell them? A story, most likely. Or what did you say when you saw that friend you had not seen for years? Didn't you swap stories of the years since you last met?

Most of us tell some stories each day, even if it is just to let a spouse or friend know how our day has gone. Storytelling comes so naturally to us that most of us don't realize that we are practicing the same art that brought us the stories of the Bible.

Why Tell Stories?

As teachers of children, you tell Bible stories as naturally as talking to your closest friend. The goal of telling Bible stories is to show, through the ancient narratives of faith, God's presence in the students' lives today. Keep in mind that storytelling in the classroom is not performance or entertainment; biblical storytelling is acquainting listeners with biblical family and deepening the loving relationship you have already begun with your students. Most important, you are deepening each student's relationship with God.

When you tell Bible stories to your students, you
• let them know that they belong to the family of faith;
• provide companions for their spiritual journey;
• provide them with the basic content of faith through examples of God's creative presence with our ancestors;
• and let them see God's creative presence in their own lives.

As the storyteller, you are serving as tour guide through the ancient world of the Bible. Although many of you may feel more comfortable in the role of teacher than in the role of storyteller, you each bring all the necessary tools; all you need is a body, a voice, and an imagination! Without your guidance and knowledge your students will miss the incredible sights, sounds, smells, and experiences. Be sure each story you tell invites their senses. And don't worry! Much of the information you will need can be found in the lesson material, but sometimes it will be helpful to look at a Bible dictionary, commentary, or other biblical reference book to help identify characters, objects, and customs of particular interest.

Using Your Imagination

Your imagination as a storyteller can spark the imaginations of your students. The information you gather from the lesson, a Bible dictionary, or a laymen's guide can help create the world of the story. Don't be afraid to embellish the story with details that "might have been." Give students enough information to imagine for themselves. Imagination simply involves offering enough detail for your listener to actively participate in creating the story world. The artistry is in giving enough detail without overdoing it, and without getting bogged down in too many details. You want to allow your students enough imaginative room to do their part in creating the story.

What About Gestures?

How comfortable are you with your body? Your use of movement in storytelling will depend on your comfort with your body and its range of movement. A simple gesture can show an emotion or the size of an object or the height of a character. It is always appropriate to sing a Bible story song or involve the students in acting out the story after you have told it.

Emphasize With Your Voice

Your voice is the most effective tool you have to communicate the energy and feelings for an effectively told story. If a character you are describing is happy, sad, afraid, or ashamed, your voice must communicate that. If the tone of a story is somber or suspenseful or fanciful, show it by the tone of your voice. If you are having a difficult time holding the attention of your listeners, use a trick that storytellers have employed for centuries: instead of raising your voice, speak more softly. This will draw your listeners into the story, sometimes encouraging them to literally lean in to hear more clearly.

Older Elementary Children

Older elementary children like stories! In fact, the characters and stories often seem more interesting to older elementary children when the teacher reads or tells stories aloud. The role of storytelling expands as the students get to know the members of their biblical family. The characters in these Bible stories become their familiar companions and will then accompany them through life, reminding them of their faith and of the values of those who follow the Scriptures and Jesus' teachings. When we tell stories to this age group, we are both populating and strengthening their inner world.

Bible people made real through storytelling accompany children, teens, and adults through life. When children must move out of familiar surroundings, say to a strange house and neighborhood, Abraham and Sarah will go with them. When they face their worst fears, young David will stand beside them with his

sling and five smooth stones. When they are the new kid in class, feeling very much like a foreigner, Ruth the Moabite will speak words of hope and courage. When they go off into the "far country" of disobedience and alienation, Jesus' prodigal son will whisper words of forgiveness and home, and they will look for the welcoming father figure.

Older elementary children can deal with more of the content of faith than younger children. This may include the historical or cultural background that can be found either in the lesson or any good Bible dictionary or a resource like *The Storyteller's Companion to the Bible* (Abingdon). To complement the story, encourage the students to put the story into action by constructing scale model buildings of the period, making costumes, and acting out the story.

We know that stories shape decision-making. We Christians are a people with a specific set of stories that we claim are sacred to us. Those stories are contained in the Bible. The choices we make are a reflection of the stories we live. So our ethics take shape as we learn the stories of our faith tradition. Stories that are not from the Bible, but are drawn from the history of the people of faith, can also be helpful as we are formed in the peculiar people God has called us to become.

Perhaps the most important thing to remember in telling Bible stories to persons of any age is that, as Christians, the story we have to tell is a love story. We are like children on the playground passing along a love note to a beloved child that reads "Did you know God loves you?" This is our calling: To tell stories about the God who loves all of us to people we have come to love. This is also one of the greatest privileges anyone can have.

Adapted from "Telling Bible Stories," by Michael Williams, *Children's Teacher*, Summer 1997.

Bible ONE®

Bible ONE®

_____

_____

Bible ONE®

Bible ONE®

_____

_____

Bible ONE®

Bible ONE®

_____

_____

Bible ONE®

Bible ONE®

_____

_____

The Bible Zone

Where else can we find a lesson learned on every page?
Stories that have lived to teach us all from age to age.
From the flood to parting waters, burning bushes,
  prophets, scholars,
God's Word takes us anywhere.

In the Bible Zone where God's Word come to life.
In the Bible Zone our path is always bright.
A book for all creation to every boy and girl.
In the Bible Zone is God's treasure for the world.

Learning of forgiveness or when learning how to pray,
God's word gives examples of the things we face each day
When we choose to look inside we see ahead or back in time.
God's word takes us anywhere.

In the Bible Zone where God's Word come to life.
In the Bible Zone our path is always bright.
A book for all creation to every boy and girl.
In the Bible Zone is God's treasure for the world.

In the Bible Zone where God's Word come to life.
In the Bible Zone our path is always bright.
A book for all creation to every boy and girl.
In the Bible Zone is God's treasure for the world.

Words: David Hampton
Copyright © 1997 New Spring Publishing, Inc. (ASCAP),
A div. of Brentwood-Benson Music Publishing, Inc.
All Rights Reserved. Used by permission.

Comments
From Users

Use the following scale to rate BibleZone® resources
If you did not use a section, write "Did not use" in the Comments space.

1 = In No Lessons   2 = In Some Lessons   3 = In Most Lessons   4 = In All Lessons

1. *Enter the Zone* provided information that helped me teach this lesson's Scripture.
1   2   3   4   Comments:

2. The *Scope the Zone* chart made lesson planning easy.
1   2   3   4   Comments:

3. The teaching plan was organized in a way that made it easy to use.
1   2   3   4   Comments:

4. The Teacher's Guide provided easy-to-follow instructions for the learning activities.
1   2   3   4   Comments:

5. The supplies necessary to do the activities were easily located in my home or church.
1   2   3   4   Comments:

6. My students were able to understand the lesson's ZoneIn®.
1   2   3   4   Comments:

7. The activities matched the learning level and abilities of my students.
1   2   3   4   Comments:

8. The number of activities in the lesson plan worked for the time I had available (indicate how much time):_____.
   If not, check:_____ too many _____too few.
1   2   3   4   Comments:

9. I used activities from the "GameZone" section of the Teacher's Guide.
1   2   3   4   Comments:

10. I used activities from the "ArtZone" section of the Teacher's Guide.
1   2   3   4   Comments:

11. I used information from articles I read in the Teacher's Guide.
1   2   3   4   Comments:

12. I used the Cassette in my classroom.
1   2   3   4   Comments:

13. I used items from the BibleZone® FUNspirational® Kit
1   2   3   4   Comments:

14. I sent the HomeZone® page home to students.
1   2   3   4   Comments:

FOOTER

OLDER ELEMENTARY 7

Permission granted to photocopy for local church use. © 1999 Abingdon Press.

175

ADDITIONAL COMMENTS

Activities my students enjoy the most are:

Activities my students enjoy the least are:

I use BibleZone® for_____Sunday School _____Second Hour Sunday School _____Children's Church

_____Wednesday nights _____Sunday nights _____Children's Fellowship _____other

ABOUT MY CLASS

Number of Students at Each Age in My Class:

_____Age 9_____Age 10_____Age 11_____Age 12

_____Other (Specify)_____

Average number of students who attend my class each week:_____

I teach: _____alone _____with another teacher each week

_____taking turns with other teachers _____with an adult helper

ABOUT MY CHURCH

_____Rural _____Small Town _____Downtown _____Suburban

_____Under 200 Members _____200-700 Members _____Over 700 Members

Church Name and Address: _____

_____

My Name and Address: _____

_____

Please return this form to **Amy Smith**
Research Department
201 8th Ave., So
P.O. Box 801
Nashville, TN 37202-0801

176

To indigenous people everywhere, in gratitude for the profound gifts they've given to all of humanity.—TJM

To the Grandmothers.—WC

The
THUNDER EGG

By

Tim J. Myers

Illustrated by

Winfield Coleman

✤Wisdom Tales✤

tands-by-Herself lived with her people on the great plains, amid endless grasses and endless sky.

Her grandmother was the only family she had. The old woman had named her "Stands-by-Herself." "Your heart is different," she told her granddaughter.

But other children made fun of her. She was shy, and sometimes would go off alone. They didn't know she was thinking and dreaming.

Stands-by-Herself would find sage-grouse chicks in the waving grass.

She would gaze at the new moon. She watched the ducks overhead in autumn.

"I want to fly away with the ducks," she told her grandmother. "The duck people don't hurt each other."

"Don't listen when the children tease you," her grandmother answered. "The Creator made different kinds of people. Someday you'll find your power, and with it the good you can do in the world."

One spring day, Stands-by-Herself found an odd gray stone.

"That looks like a thunder egg!" her grandmother said. "The great Thunderbird's wife may have laid it. Perhaps she lost it."

The Thunderbird! He was the Creator's giant eagle, the rain-bringer, whose wing-flaps made thunder, whose flashing eyes made lightning.

She held the stone close. But when she showed it to the other children, they just laughed. "You can't hatch an eagle from a rock!" they shouted.

But she cared for it, making a cradle-wrap out of an old piece of tipi-cover. She made a song too:

Sleep and grow strong, my little one.
Wake and grow wise, my little one.
Someday you will be powerful.
Someday your deeds will bring joy to the people.

When summer came, the days grew hot. The grass wilted and the hunters couldn't find buffalo. Each afternoon thunderclouds formed, but no rain fell.

The people were hungry. Some got sick. Even her grandmother grew quiet and sad. The holy man said they must offer sacrifices to make the world new.

Stands-by-Herself thought about how things were. She loved the thunder egg as if it were her own child. But the people were suffering.

Finally she decided. She must give up the thunder egg.

So, brushing away tears, she took it to a high ridge near the camp. On that ridge her grandmother had once shown her a juniper struck by lightning—so the Thunderbird had come there before.

She left the egg at the foot of the tree, on a bed of pine needles, sage, and sweet grass. A great sadness burned inside her. But she climbed back down, sweating under the fierce sun.

In the night lightning came, so wild the people hid in their tipis. Only Stands-by-Herself peeked out to watch the blue-white streaks leaping down.

When she climbed the ridge the next day, she couldn't find the thunder egg. But the tree had been split to the ground, and pieces of purple crystal glowed all around it. She realized the crystal had been hidden inside the gray rock she knew so well. And she knew lightning had found the egg and shattered it.

new Thunderbird had been born! For a moment her heart ached with loneliness. But then she felt a gust of wind. The Thunderbird was coming!

Out across the vast plains she could see dark clouds streaming in from the northwest. Beneath them hung sweeping gray curves—rain!

The father bird was now happy and proud, and would shed his rain on the waiting land! The buffalo would come back for the fresh grass!

Then thunder boomed across the world, and she knew the Thunderbird was flapping closer.

Suddenly she heard a voice as big as the sky. It said:

You have cared for my child.
You have brought this blessing to your people.

s the echoes faded, she ran back down to camp. Just as she was telling everyone what happened, the first big drops began to fall.

That night, as the world was made new, happy people gathered around their fires as rain beat on their tipis. Stands-by-Herself was seated beside the chief, and all were praising her.

The elders had already begun telling the story of the girl who cared for the Thunderbird's child—and saved her people.

The End

Afterword

I grew up at the foot of Pikes Peak, where the Rocky Mountains meet the endless prairies of the Great Plains. Many of the Plains tribes spent time in Colorado, and I've been fascinated by them since early childhood. All had stories about the great Thunderbird—a being of particular power in a land that gets only ten to twenty inches of rain a year.

When I was younger, someone once showed me a geode—a rather plain-looking rock that, when cracked open, reveals crystals inside, usually of quartz, and sometimes a brilliant purple in color. This still seems to me a very magical thing.

At some point, these two fascinations began to work together in me. There were other things too. I read about the little girl who, through a vision, actually started the Cheyenne tribal council; about the Cheyenne tendency to seek union with the powers of the universe through "sacrificial offering"; about how grandparents passed down stories and traditions to young people; and about how the Thunderbird was considered the creator Maheo's bird who "brings the summer rains...," and how he was sometimes "a voice in the clouds."

All that and more was in my head when I wrote this story.

Making a geode a thunderbird egg was my own invention (the actual "thunder egg" in geology is slightly different). But the rest of the story closely follows the folktale traditions of the many Plains tribes, and is based directly on genuine information about their lives—even, for example, to the use of cradle-wraps, and of sage and sweet grass as part of spiritual life.

But my hope is that this story, like the many great stories the Plains people still tell, will reach much further, since it's really about things we can all understand simply by being human. The idea of sacrifice seems to have been as important to the Cheyenne as it was to the Catholicism of my youth—and everyone must learn that we sometimes come to our greatest power for good when we truly give of ourselves.

—Tim J. Myers

Notes on the Illustrations

1. The cover: The story takes place before horses were introduced to the Cheyenne. Stands-by-Herself wears a side-fold dress, used in the early 18th century (cf. McLaughlin 2003:107 ff.). The red paint on the part of her hair represents the sun's path.

Before the story begins:

2. The end papers (front and back): Monarch butterflies, known as "Red Messengers," are associated with thunder (Moore 1986).

3. Facing the half-title page (and on the back cover): A thunderbird shield, based on a Cheyenne design.

4. The half-title page: A view of a winter camp. Fetching wood was one of the many tasks assigned to women and girls, in all weather.

5. The dedication page: A Western Meadowlark. The black crescent on its breast associates it with the moon, while the yellow color is emblematic of the sun.

6. The title page: A Thunderbird.

The story:

7. Page 4 (first page of story text): Sage grouse chicks.

8. Page 5: Stands-by-Herself carries a digging stick and a painted rawhide bag for collecting wild turnips—some of which bloom at her feet. The small bag around her neck contains her umbilical cord.

9. Page 6: The V-shaped formations of flying ducks relate to a common design element in women's embroidery. This is a reminder to follow society's leaders and not to step out of line: every member must do his or her part to foster cultural cohesion (Lukavic 2013:4).

10. Page 8 (behind the initial letter): Cattails.

11. Page 9: Stands-by-Herself and her grandmother. Her grandmother must be a person of standing and resourcefulness, to survive with her granddaughter and no male relatives. Stands-by-Herself cradles the Thunder Egg in a small version of a traditional Cheyenne cradle-wrap.

12. Page 10: Vultures (behind the initial letter) and a buffalo skull.

13. Page 11: The holy man. His coiled hair and body paint indicate he is a thunder shaman. He carries a Straight Pipe, to signify he is speaking in his official capacity as a man of knowledge and a seer (Coleman Field Notes 9.26.97, 7.5.98 & 9.26.98; Dunn 1969; cf. Thomas & Ronnefeldt 1976:132). Freshwater pearl shells, which hang from his ears, were prized from the earliest periods, and have been found in Moundbuilder sites: "We use a shell [in ceremonies] to reflect all the beauty in the earth and universe" (Coleman Field Notes 9.26.12, 9.26.97).

14. Page 13 (behind the initial letter): Ponderosa pine cones.

15. Page 14 (behind the initial letter): A prairie rose flower.

16. Page 15: Juniper trees were considered sacred to Thunder, as they are especially prone to be struck by lightning. Thunder's nest is "in the cedar [i.e. juniper] of the western mountains" (Gilmore 1991:11).

17. Page 16 (behind the initial letter): Little Wood Satyr butterflies (*megisto cymela*) are called "Thunder's lice" by the Cheyenne, as they are noted for flying about in storms, when other butterflies seek shelter. They are also known to drink blood (Coleman Field Notes 9.22.99-9.24.99; cf. Grinnell 1972 II:95).

18. Page 17: "The Thunder often appears as a great bird, somewhat like an eagle, but much larger" (Grinnell 1972 II:95).

19. Page 18: A chief's large tipi was sometimes made from two or even more covers, to accommodate an assemblage.

20. Page 19: Running buffalo.

After the story ends:

21. Page 20 (opposite the Afterword): The very old design on these moccasins represents a buffalo pound and the Evening Star; the design also represents the interior of a lodge, and a camp circle (Coleman 1980: 56-7; Coleman Field Notes 7.2.83; cf. Lukavic 2013:54-55). Impoundment (driving prey into a circular corral) was the principal means of hunting buffalo before the arrival of the horse.

22. Page 23 (Notes on the Illustrations): The three crosses on the blanket strip may represent the belt in the constellation of Orion, forming part of a Cheyenne constellation (which includes Sirius) referred to as the White Buffalo. The heliacal rising of Sirius, the White Star, signaled the beginning of the Buffalomen Rite, which was especially concerned with the buffalo hunt. This design is known as the Morning Star Design (Coleman Field Notes 9.22.12; Schlesier 1987: 84).

23. Page 25 (the copyright page): A badger. The spiritually powerful badger is used to communicate to the Underworld powers (Grinnell 1972 II:105). For example, a badger skin is sometimes put on the roof of a sweat lodge to convey prayers underground; a badger skin is used in Arrow ceremonies (Coleman Field Notes 6.18.95).

—**Winfield Coleman**

Bibliography

Coleman, Winfield. Field Notes, 1978-2013.

————. 1980. "The Cheyenne Women's Sewing Society." In *Plains Indian Design Symbology and Decoration*, edited by Gene Ball and George P. Horse Capture. Cody: Buffalo Bill Historical Center.

————. 1998. "Art as Cosmology: Cheyenne Women's Rawhide Painting." *The World of Tribal Arts* V (1).

Dunn, Dorothy. 1969. *1877: Plains Indian Sketch Books of Zo-Tom & Howling Wolf*. Flagstaff: Northland Press.

Gilmore, Melvin R. 1991. *Uses of Plants by the Indians of the Missouri River Region*. Lincoln: University of Nebraska Press.

Grinnell, George Bird. 1972. *The Cheyenne Indians: Their History and Way of Life*. 2 vols. Lincoln: University of Nebraska Press.

Lukavic, John. 2013. "Teaching a Nation: Transmitting Knowledge through Southern Cheyenne Art." *American Indian Art* Magazine XXXVIII (3), Summer.

McLaughlin, Castle. 2003. *Arts of Diplomacy: Lewis & Clark's Indian Collection*. Seattle: University of Washington Press.

Moore, John H. 1986. "The Ornithology of Cheyenne Religionists." *Plains Anthropologist* XXXI (113):177-192.

Schlesier, Karl H. 1987. *The Wolves of Heaven: Cheyenne Shamanism, Ceremonies, and Prehistoric Origins*. Norman: University of Oklahoma Press.

Thomas, Davis and Karin Ronnefeldt. 1976. *People of the First Man: Life Among the Plains Indians in Their Final Days of Glory*. New York: E. P. Dutton.

The Thunder Egg
Text copyright © 2015 Tim J. Myers, Illustrations copyright © 2015 Winfield Coleman

Book design by Stephen Williams.
Wisdom Tales is an imprint of World Wisdom, Inc.

Printed in China on acid-free paper.
Production Date: February 2015, Plant & Location: Printed by 1010 Printing International Ltd,
Job/Batch # TT15010455
Library of Congress Cataloging-in-Publication Data
Myers, Tim, 1953- author.
 The thunder egg / by Tim J. Myers ; illustrated by Winfield Coleman.
   pages cm
  ISBN 978-1-937786-39-7 (casebound : alk. paper) 1. Cheyenne Indians--Colorado-
-Juvenile fiction. [1. Cheyenne Indians--Fiction. 2. Indians of North America--Colorado--
Fiction. 3. Sacrifice--Fiction.] I. Coleman, Winfield, illustrator. II. Title.
 PZ7.M57195Th 2015
 [E]--dc23
                                                                    2014048330
For information address Wisdom Tales, P.O. Box 2682, Bloomington, Indiana 47402-2682
www.wisdomtalespress.com